INSIDER SECRETS TO SELLING YOUR BUSINESS

MAXIMIZE PRICE
WITH SEAMLESS TRANSITION

———

Joshua D. Sagman
Hillel L. Presser, Esq., MBA

INSIDER SECRETS TO SELLING YOUR BUSINESS: Maximize Price with Seamless Transition

Copyright © 2024 by Brookline Press, LLC

Printed in the USA by Brookline Press, LLC

DEDICATION

To the courageous business owners who dared to dream, took risks, and built something extraordinary: Your unwavering dedication to your vision inspires. Let this book be a guiding light on your journey to selling your business with grace, maximizing its value, and ensuring a seamless transition to the next chapter.

To the beloved family members, whose steadfast support and understanding have been the cornerstone of our endeavors: Your love, patience, and encouragement have fueled our passion. This book is dedicated to you, with heartfelt gratitude for being our unwavering source of strength and inspiration.

TABLE OF CONTENTS

FOREWORD

In the ever-changing landscape of business, there are few endeavors as daunting and rewarding as selling your business. As someone who has experienced the highs and lows of the business world, I know firsthand the significance of this journey. That's why I'm thrilled to introduce: "Insider Secrets to Selling Your Business: Maximize Price with Seamless Transition".

Authored by Hillel Presser and Josh Sagman, trusted experts in the field of business brokerage, this book is jammed packed with invaluable insights, strategies, and, yes, insider secrets. But what truly sets it apart is its genuine commitment to the business owner spirit.

Throughout these pages, you'll find not only practical advice on maximizing the value of your business and ensuring a seamless transition, but also a deep understanding of the emotional and personal stakes involved in this process.

As "The People's Shark", I've always believed that success is not just about financial gains, but also about creating meaningful impact and leaving a legacy. And in that spirit, this book is a beacon of empowerment for every business owner embarking on the next chapter of their journey.

So, whether you're a seasoned entrepreneur looking to unlock the full potential of your business or a visionary leader contemplating your next move, "Insider Secrets to Selling Your Business" is your indispensable guide. Here's to your success, your legacy, and the next chapter of your remarkable story.

-Daymond John

The People's Shark

INTRODUCTION

One thing all business owners must understand on some level is sales. Even if it's been decades since you were directly involved in getting customers to buy the products or services you offer, you understand that without buyers your business would cease to exist. What should you do when you're ready to stop selling to customers and instead want to put a "For Sale" sign on your business? If you're smart, the first thing you do is pick up this book.

This is not a "How-to" book that will teach you how to sell your business. Instead, it is a guide designed to help you find and recruit the right team - to do the hard work for you. Utilizing carefully curated information about what it takes to sell a business from our years of doing just that, combined with simple and specially designed exercises at the end of each chapter, the goal of this book is to give you the foundational tools necessary to feel confident with preparing for your sale.

Section 1: *So, you think you can sell?, Pt.1* guides you through an assessment to determine whether or not you're positioned to sell your business; while also providing insight on what to do if you find you're not.

Section 2: *Before the "For Sale"* focuses on what an average business owner needs to have in place to take their business to market.

Section 3: *The Art of the Sale* addresses the specific aspects of a business sale.

Section 4: *So, you think you can sell?, Pt. 2,* concentrates on business owners who are positioned to sell their business(es) and provides insight on steps to take to protect themselves financially, once the sale is complete.

SO, YOU THINK YOU CAN SELL? PT. 1

Are you ready to sell your business? Before answering "yes", think about what, in this exact moment, you know about selling a business in today's marketplace. Unlike selling a product or a service, or even unloading assets from the company or real estate associated with it, the process of business brokering has unique challenges (and rewards) that need to be carefully considered. When you're selling a business, you must look beyond the act of what you're doing, and the reasons you're doing it, to focus on what it is that you're truly offering a potential buyer. This requires an in-depth understanding of your business from an objective viewpoint.

This section will focus on assessing your readiness to sell your business. When you're finished reading this section, you'll be able to do all the following:

- Tell the difference between the perceived, potential, and real value of your business based on its current ownership, size, and structure.
- Know the importance of having a plan in place to sell; and what the basic aspects of that plan should be.
- Understand how to clean up your books and records to reflect your readiness to sell your business.

1. BUSINESS CHECK-IN

"Do what you can, with what you have, where you are." - Theodore Roosevelt

Being able to talk about your business clearly, concisely, and accurately is one of the most important skills a business owner can have. It's also incredibly important when thinking about selling your business because it places a clear focus on basic facts that can, and more importantly, will be checked out by any serious buyer. Without hesitation, you need to be able to present your business mission, its size and scope, , its current ownership structure, and its perceived worth. These may seem like straightforward and simple tasks, but that's not always the case. So, it's better to work out your answers now *before* your business is taken to market to avoid unnecessary delays or unpleasant surprises.

Business size and ownership matter

When it comes to selling a business, size definitely matters, but so do factors such as current positioning and possible future scalability. This shouldn't be misconstrued to mean that bigger will always be better or that international or global companies, (or those that can be scaled internationally or globally) have an inherent edge over local or regional ones. Instead, it's a clear call to assess what your business really looks like in terms of its market reach right now. One way to do this is to determine whether your business can be most accurately categorized as being a main street business, a middle-market business, or something else entirely.

What is a main street business?

The term main street business may initially conjure up images of business type versus business size. This perspective isn't wrong, as main street businesses are oftentimes local businesses that are easily recognizable within a community. Businesses like hair salons, local insurance offices, and restaurants are all good examples, and with good reason. This is because these types of businesses are historically brick and mortar locations that are literally located on the main street of an area or in the middle of a small town. Currently, the largest percentage of these types of businesses are owned by Baby Boomers. Why is this important? It's simple. This generation is at retirement age and coupled with their potential willingness to leave the business world behind for a life of leisure, means they are most likely to sell their businesses. Even if this doesn't describe your exact situation, there are still some key facts that you need to know about selling a main street business.

In the context of selling a business, it's less about the specific goods or services your business offers and more about how much your company generates in annual sales. A prime reason for this is that businesses have evolved over time, and a main street business no longer needs to be physically located on a main street, nor does it need to provide the products or services that are typically associated with these types of businesses. Therefore, at Business Exit Advisors, we classify any company that does between $250k and $8million in annual sales as a main street business. Based on this revenue range, main street businesses may not always be the most obvious or accessible to the public and can also include companies that do wholesaling, import-exporting, or niche services.

It's important to understand when trying to sell a main street business that what's traditional in this space doesn't always translate into the most profit. For example, retail stores, which are quintessential main street businesses, are one of the hardest types of businesses to sell. Why is this the case? The answer has to do with Seller's Discretionary Earnings, or SDE which is the amount of money that a business owner pulls out of their business on an annual basis to run their business. Any money that is expensed through the business that isn't directly related to the business operations such as cell phone bills, or any personal charges on a credit card would be added back into the business revenues as income. Once adjusted, that final bottom line earnings will be multiplied by a number in range with the comparable businesses in structure, size, and industry. While a retail store may sell at a 1.5 multiple, a strong IT company can sell at a 8-10 times multiple of Seller Discretionary Earnings. What this means, is that the IT company is ultimately viewed as being more valuable even though its services may be far more niche than that of something like a clothing boutique or hair salon. Keeping this in mind, it's beneficial not to make assumptions about the potential value of your business based primarily on factors like your longevity or specific goods or services you offer.

What is a middle-market business?

Middle-market businesses are more varied than main street businesses. This can be true in terms of both the type of operation as well as in the range of annual sales. While main street businesses are often thought of in terms of those that may be specific to a certain community; businesses classified as middle-market are generally larger firms that may have greater name recognition or industry significance based on their size and the number of products or services they provide. The exact clarification of a medium or large size business can, and does, differ and is dependent on factors including industry, location, and market condition.

At Business Exit Advisors, we classify any company that does between $8mm and $50mm in sales as being a middle-market business. Based on these figures, middle-market businesses are more likely to be companies that operate beyond their local or regional area and will generally have a combination of a brick and mortar and online presence or an online only presence along with a serious support team to operate a business of this size.

How does Business Exit Advisors handle a larger business or one that is the result of mergers and acquisitions?

While all businesses sold by Business Exit Advisors receive full expert attention, businesses that do over $50mm in sales or those that are the result of mergers and acquisitions need to be handled a little differently than main street businesses or middle-market businesses. The reason for this is that larger businesses, or those that were formed following a merger or taken over in an acquisition, often have unique needs that can require the input of additional specialists on the team. These specialists help to ensure that everything is handled properly.

Why does business size matter?

Knowing whether your business can be classified as a main street business, a middle-market business, or something outside of those two main categories is key for a business broker. This is because it helps us determine critical factors such as the best potential pool of buyers, what specific documentation will be required, and how financing will ideally work. Essentially, this information is foundational to positioning your business for a successful sale.

Who owns your business?

The question of who owns your business is one that will be determined in large part by how your business is structured, and what type of business you have. For example, if you're a sole proprietor then your business structure is likely a lot more simplified than that of a franchisee for a major chain, or even the co-owner of a family business. In the latter cases, your personal desire to sell may not be sufficient as you may need to consult with or get permission from others. While Business Exit Advisors will certainly assist you in navigating these more complex ownership situations, it's incredibly helpful if we're aware upfront of what potential issues may exist that could slow down the sales process.

Basic types of business ownership

In general, there are 5 main types of business ownership. These include sole proprietorships, partnerships, Limited Liability Companies (LLCs), corporations and franchises. Each of these ownership structures are defined by 3 characteristics including the ownership rules, the liability, and the way in which they're taxed. Chances are good that you're already clear on how your business is owned, but if there's even a little bit of doubt about it, or what types of rights you may have when it comes to selling your business, then it's far better to double, and even triple check, if necessary. Taking the time to ensure you're clear on how your business is owned can help you to avoid potential confusion and frustration later.

Sole Proprietorships

First, the simplest type of business ownership is sole proprietorship. At Business Exit Advisors we refer to these as owner-operated businesses. As the name suggests, these are any businesses that are owned by a single person. As a result, a person who owns this type of business has unlimited personal liability and is taxed with self-employment taxes and personal taxes.

There are clear benefits to this type of ownership when looking to sell the business. The most important one is that the only person who needs to be willing to make the sale is you. Additionally, minus any fees that need to be paid out, you're the sole or primary beneficiary of the proceeds of the sale. However, this doesn't necessarily mean that selling these types of businesses is easy.

One of the biggest problems with owner operated businesses is the fact that the owner is the primary or even sole provider of goods and services and may work 60+ hours a week to ensure that the business runs to their standards. When this type of business is sold though, the owner is ultimately replaced. As an example of this, Business Exit Advisors was responsible for handling the sale of a dog grooming facility in Boca Raton, Florida. The facility was a popular destination for celebrities, athletes and Fortune 500 business owner clients who were all very particular about the way their dogs were cared for and placed their trust in the owner who was also the groomer. To help ensure that the sale of the business didn't result in an automatic loss of clientele, it was necessary for a clear transition agreement to be included as a part of the sale. Per this agreement, the seller stayed on for a period of 90 days following the sale. This allowed the buyer, who was not a groomer by trade, to bring in a groomer for the business who essentially apprenticed under the former owner and was warmly introduced to the high-end client list. This arrangement was what was best for all parties in this situation, and based on your current business structure and what you offer, you may need to consider if, as a seller, you're willing to make a similar concession.

Another potential issue with the sale of owner-operated businesses is related to liability and taxation. This may never be an issue for you. This may never become an issue for you, but it is important that you are aware of strategies some sellers use during a sale to avoid financial obligations that could lead to unwanted legal attention.

Partnerships

Partnerships, unfortunately, aren't always straightforward in terms of business ownership. Every partnership is made up of two or more people, all of whom have unlimited personal liability unless the partnership is structured as a limited partnership. All partners, except for limited partners are responsible for self-employment taxes, and personal taxes. Regardless of the stake owned in the business, if all partners agree to sell, there generally isn't an issue. Where problems may arise, however, is if the partners aren't all in agreement about the sale itself or the process that it should follow. This is true even if the person or partners with the majority share are in favor of selling. In this case, there are certainly situations where issues can be resolved amicably among the members of the partnership without intervention by a third party.

LLCs

The ownership of an LLC is based on its membership, and as such, decisions about the sale of a business are influenced by that. While the formation of a LLC means that owners are not personally liable, the self-employment taxation along with personal taxes or corporate taxes may mean that the sale of a business owned by an LLC is more heavily scrutinized for legitimacy in terms of ensuring that assets are not being reassigned to avoid tax burdens. Additionally, similar to partnerships, there is a need to ensure that all members of the LLC have agreed both to the sale of the business and the terms under which it is taking place. This is a situation where having knowledgeable business brokers is key.

Corporations

Corporations can represent the trickiest business sales if the brokers aren't experienced. The reason for this is that there are multiple types of corporate structures, including C Corps, S Corps, B Corps and non-profit corporations. Ownership for all of these requires one or more owners, none of whom must assume personal liability. It should be noted that S Corps ownership can't be held by more than 100 people and all of them must be U.S. citizens. For both C Corps and B Corps the taxes are corporate while for S Corps taxes are personal. Non-profit corporations are tax exempt but corporate profits can't be distributed.

A special note about partnerships, LLCs and corporations

At Business Exit Advisors the vast majority (95%) of the work we do involves selling the assets of the business. What this means for owners of partnerships, LLCs, and corporations is that at the sale the entity of the seller is dissolved, and the buyers create a new entity that owns the business. This is an efficient and effective way to ensure that both the parties selling the business and those buying it are afforded a fresh start, assuring that there is little public confusion about who actually owns the business.

Franchises

Finally, focus needs to be placed on franchises. If you're a business owner who is also a franchisee then the rights, you have may differ from those of someone whose business is structured in another way because you must account for what the franchisor will and will not allow. To determine this, careful attention will need to be paid to the franchise documents. While all this documentation is important, what is especially relevant is the Franchise Disclosure Document and the Franchise Agreement. The Franchise Disclosure Document outlines crucial information about the franchise opportunity. In general, this includes, but isn't limited to, providing details about the franchise fee, royalties, training, and territory. The Franchise Agreement effectively codifes the information contained in the Franchise Disclosure Document, because it's the legally binding document that establishes the terms and conditions that govern the franchise. While these are documents that you generally go over before your franchise ownership begins, Business Exit Advisors thoroughly reviews this paperwork to determine the viability of the transfer or sale of the franchise.

Why does business ownership matter?

Before you start the process of selling your business it's essential that you're certain about ownership and who, other than you, may be entitled to input. The rationale for why this is important is simple; you can't legally sell something that isn't yours or that you haven't been explicitly authorized to sell no matter what your reasons or intentions are. If there's the slightest bit of uncertainty about corporate ownership, take the time to check it out.

What is your business really worth?

In many ways, what a business is worth is subjective based on who's being asked and how they're assessing that value. For example, the owner of a new business who has invested a significant amount of their own capital and sweat equity may utilize these factors and the size of their industry to justify a valuation that differs drastically from that of a potential purchaser of that same business who is utilizing more objective information, like sales figures. While it's important to understand the potential value that a business has, it's also important to have a clear accounting of what the actual value of a business has at the time that it's being taken to market.

At Business Exit Advisors, each business valuation is handled on a case-by-case basis using verifiable financial information. This is a process that will be discussed in-depth in Chapter 4. For now, what's important to understand is that the value of the business is less about its possible future potential and more about its current assets, profits, and debts.

Exercises for Moving Forward

At the start of this chapter, it was presented that being able to talk about your business clearly, concisely, and accurately is one of the most important skills that any business owner can have. Building upon that, complete the following sentences as if you're having your first consultation with Business Exit Advisors. Some of the questions that you're answering at this juncture will be repeated in later chapters, and it is likely that as you gain additional insight you may see differences in the responses you provide. Taking the time to make comparisons between the variations in answers will showcase which, if any, of your feelings or priorities have shifted, and ultimately allow you to make the most informed decision about how to move forward with the sale of your business and who you trust to assist you in that process.

1. I am the owner of a _____ business (fill in the blank with main stream or middle-market or indicate whether your business is the result of a merger or acquisition). The annual sales of the business during the last fiscal year were _____ (fill in the blank with the dollar amount). My annual Seller's Discretionary Earnings are

_____.

2. My business is structured as a _____ (fill in the blank with the ownership structure). Based on this structure I think the biggest benefit is _____.
However, I am concerned about _____.
Based on this, I would like the help of Business Exit Advisors to

_____.

3. I *perceive* the value of my business to be _____ (fill in the blank with the dollar amount). My basis for this valuation is _____

_____.

The *potential* value for this business within the next year is _____ (fill in the blank with the dollar amount). My basis for this valuation is

_____.

The current *real* value of my business based on its total assets minus its total liabilities is _____ (fill in the blank with the dollar amount).

4. Ideally, I'd like to receive _____ (fill in the blank with the dollar amount) for my business. I think that this amount is a reasonable asking price because _____.

       Keep in mind that the answers that you provided above may change as you move forward with the process of selling your business. Not only is this completely okay, but it's expected. The reason for this is that the more you learn about the process of selling a business, the greater the likelihood that your perspective about some, or even all, aspects of it will change. At Business Exit Advisors, we're with you every step of the way to support you and help you navigate your evolving thoughts and feelings about selling your business.

       Now that you've completed your business check-in, it's time to examine necessary business selling basics.

2. BUSINESS SELLING BASICS

"Selling is really about having conversations with people and helping improve their company or their life." - Lori Richardson

Selling a business can be a complex process, but it doesn't have to be. One of the easiest ways to limit the possible challenges you may face is by hiring the right business brokers for you, your business, and other interests that you've identified as being pertinent to the deal. Determining which business broker to work with should ideally start with understanding the basics of business selling. Specifically, you need to be clear about the exact role that a business broker is supposed to play as a part of the process of selling your business, and you should be involved with the steps they plan on taking to help you move forward. The most important thing to remember though is that whoever you choose to hire should work with you in a way that helps you to feel secure that your needs (both business and personal) are being met and your voice is being heard.

Business Brokerage basics

One of the most important pieces of information for anyone looking to work with a business broker is to understand exactly what it is a business broker is supposed to do for them. While not all business brokers work the exact same way, there are some things that anyone claiming to be a business broker should be doing. The key is to find business brokers who perform these tasks well, and ideally those who have a proven track record of working with businesses like yours.

In the broadest sense, the role of a business broker is to help their client buy or sell a business. When focused on the sales aspect this goes well beyond putting up a "for sale" sign and hoping for the best in terms of potential buyers coming to them. Instead, competent, and reputable business brokers perform 3 integrated tasks to help facilitate a sale for their client. These tasks include working with the business owner or owners to assess the business, collecting up to date records on the business along with other relevant information for prospective buyers, and taking the business to market. While business owners should have a clear understanding of what it is that they're offering for sale, what it's worth, and how that worth can be proved, business brokers not only double check that information but can also help to position the business in front of buyers that may be most interested in it. It's in this way that business brokers play a critical role in ensuring the business for sale is presented in a way that's not only accurate, but also flattering, to those who may be interested in purchasing it.

In addition to preparing the business for the market and facilitating its sale, business brokers can also take on an advisory role with their clients. In this capacity, business brokers may provide business owners with insight into the different offers being received as well as updates on pertinent developments. This advice is provided to business owners as a way of helping them to make the decision that ultimately proves to be the best one for them.

In terms of the role of business brokers there may be questions as to why this isn't a process business owners do for themselves. The answer is twofold. First, "Yes" there are things that a business owner can do for themselves but it's unlikely that they'll be as successful as a business broker in finding the right buyer and closing the deal. Hiring a professional can help ensure expanded access to buyers through personal and business connections and brokerage communities. This may result in ensuring that a business receives offers closer to the desired sales price and may expedite the process. Second, a business owner needs to focus on maintaining business operations at their peak performance so that they can sell their business for the best price possible. If a business owner switched their focus to a potential sale they could negatively impact business operations and waste time with the wrong buyer

How to find the right business brokers?

Finding the right business broker to handle your sale depends largely on what it is that you're looking for. Similar to searching for multiple vendors or service providers before deciding which one to ultimately utilize, don't be afraid to look into different business brokerages to find the brokers that are the best suited for you and your business. While all business brokers are essentially supposed to perform the same function, they may do it in drastically different ways, and these differences can heavily influence the experience that you have.

How does Business Exit Advisors make a difference?

It's impossible within the scope of this book to provide information about every business brokerage currently in operation. What it is possible to do is highlight what differentiates Business Exit Advisors from other business brokers.

Most importantly Business Exit Advisors focuses only on the Business of selling your business. Why is this important? Simple, it means that all we do is help owners sell their companies. It's how we excel at finding the best buyer and getting the best sale terms. If we need to engage with another aspect of the industry, we gladly refer that work out to other trusted specialists.. In contrast, there are other brokerages that use their real estate licenses to provide different types of services. What this means is that instead of selling businesses everyday it's not uncommon for them to also be selling houses or engaging in commercial real estate deals. This doesn't necessarily make the brokers who work at these brokerages bad at their jobs, but it does mean that business sales aren't their sole focus, or even their primary focus, which can limit the types of prospective buyers and protract the sales process.

Another defining aspect of Business Exit Advisors is our stellar team. The team at Business Exit Advisors is comprised of business broker superstars. One clear example of this can be found when looking at the owner. Before the founding of Business Exit Advisors Joshua Sagman worked at the largest business brokerage in the world and while there was one of the top producers earning the prestigious President's Club Award every year he was with the company. Additionally, he's called upon for his extensive industry knowledge and has given hundreds of presentations, has been a keynote speaker at several conventions and was at one point in charge of training other brokers. Finally, his diligence and skill has been formally recognized in his receipt of numerous other awards including the TOP 50 Business Broker in the State of Florida by the (BBF) Business Brokers of Florida, along with being presented with the Million Dollar plus Award. He was also recently acknowledged by the IBBA (International Business Brokers Association) with the exclusive Deal Maker and Chairmans Circle Award. As a company, Business Exit Advisors has active and good standing membership in the 3 largest business brokerage organizations in the World: IBBA (International Business Broker's Association), M&A Source, and locally the Business Brokers of Florida. This personal experience and recognition, along with the connections of the business itself have not only allowed Business Exit

Advisors to develop a positive reputation but also has positioned the company to assemble a team with the single goal of working with business owners (just like you) to sell their businesses in the best possible way. We get businesses in front of an unparalleled number of qualified buyers, ready to buy, even before going to market.

Finally, Business Exit Advisors works with each client to make them feel like their most important client. This is achieved by refusing to do work that isn't individualized, customized, and tailored to meet the specific needs of every business owner who has entrusted us with the sale of their business, all accomplished while educating the client every step of the way. We don't consider our jobs complete when the business sells. Instead, we work closely with our clients to ensure that we are a trusted advisor in all aspects of the business sale process. Therefore, in addition to the sale we consider the financial, taxation, estate planning, asset protection, business succession planning, and accounting points of view.

7 steps for selling a business

While every business client, and by extension every business sale, is unique and some steps aren't necessarily universal, there are some steps that must always be followed. At Business Exit Advisors we've identified 7 steps associated with all our business sales. These steps are as followed:

1. Exit Strategy 101
2. Conducting a business valuation
3. Helping clients to choose the right broker
4. Packaging the listing
5. Taking the business to market
6. Finding the right buyer
7. Closing the deal.

Much of this information is so expansive that it requires its own chapters to be fully discussed. However, there are two steps that can be explained in brief. Specifically, at this juncture we will focus on steps 1 and 4.

Exit Strategy 101 (Step 1)

Can you sell your business without a plan? Of course you can. However, it's strongly recommended that you don't try to do so. Business Exit Advisors understands that your specific plan must account for a variety of factors. These factors will include the type of business you have, what exactly you're looking to get out of the sale, and the business brokers that you're using. Just like every business is different, every plan should be different as well.

At Business Exit Advisors, we utilize what we refer to as Exit Strategy 101 as the basis for all our plans. Rather than following a one-size-fits all approach, Exit Strategy 101 is a complimentary preliminary strategy session. Offered to all our potential clients, we use this time to have a one-on-one conversation with business owners about themselves and their impending business sale. During this step, we discuss what seller's should be doing to best structure the sale of their business regardless of whether they're looking to sell today, tomorrow, or even 10 years from now.

Packaging a listing (Step 4)

At Business Exit Advisors, the process of packaging a listing for sale is one that we have mastered. For every client, we create a Confidential Information Memorandum (CIM) tailored specifically for the business. The length of the CIM can be anywhere from 10-12 pages for mainstream businesses and up to 50 pages when dealing with middle-market businesses or other larger companies. To accurately complete this document, we meet with all our clients and fill out a seller interview. This interview includes both a background on the business and the most up to date financial information for the company. If at any point during the process there are questions, concerns, or a need for further clarification, we're there for you to ensure that not only are you comfortable with the process but also that we're creating the most accurate CIM possible. Your company's CIM will serve as the foundation for the sale moving forward.

As you continue to familiarize yourself with the process associated with selling a business, what will become apparent is that the smaller steps are just as, if not more, important than the more in-depth ones. The reason for this is that every single step is necessary to ensure a sales process that maximizes a positive outcome. The steps prior to the business going to market are foundational in ensuring the accuracy of what is being offered.

How long does a sale take?

For anyone thinking about selling their business one of the first questions that comes to mind might center around how long the process takes. The most honest answer is unfortunately the most unsatisfying one because the reality is that it varies. Business Exit Advisors will always be upfront with our clients about this. Through our years of experience, we've learned about the way in which business size, business ownership, sales technique, and seller behavior can influence finding a buyer and the length of time for the sale to take place.

The role of business size

The size of a business can play a role in how long the sales process takes. At Business Exit Advisors, we have found that on average it takes between 8-10 months to sell a main street business and between 12-18 months to sell a middle-market business. The time it takes to sell a business which is the result of a merger or acquisition or a business that is a franchise can be less predictable.

The role of business ownership

As explored in the previous chapter knowing your business ownership is crucial. One reason for this is that while the way a business is owned generally doesn't impact the time that it takes to sell a business, there is a possibility that timing may be impacted if all owners aren't in agreement with the terms. Similarly, in looking at businesses that have succession plans in place, or businesses that, for whatever reason, may have specific stipulations (things like who can sell the business), there may be special considerations that have to be taken into account by business brokers to ensure that whatever work is done to sell a business will result in a legally recognized sale.

The role of how a business is sold

The question of how a business is sold may seem like a strange one when taken at face value. However, there is more than one way that a sale can be accomplished. For example, one common way that main street businesses are sold is via asset purchase agreements. What this means is that as a business owner you're not actually selling your business, you're selling the assets of the company. Once the assets are purchased, the seller's corporation is dissolved, and the buyer forms a new corporation which now owns the assets of the business. One of the main reasons buyers are interested in making asset purchases is because it means they won't be responsible for legal issues that took taking place prior to the sale of the business.

While asset purchase agreements are common, they aren't the only way businesses are sold. Businesses can also be sold as a stock sale or for E2 or EB5 visas. These types of sales may be necessary for larger companies or companies where it's legally stipulated that a sale needs to occur in such a way.

From the perspective of a business owner, how your business is sold matters. The reason for this is that stock sales or those for E2 or EB5 visas can take longer than sales that are done via asset purchase agreements. As a matter of comparison an asset purchase sale may take only 30 days or so, whereas a stock or visa sale can take much longer to complete in order to ensure that all of the appropriate parties and entities are contacted and that from a legal standpoint the new owner is not only aware of anything that happened with or to the business prior to its acquisition but that they will have protections available to them. While business sales involving stocks or visas do take longer, keep in mind that in situations where they are necessary or desired, Business Exit Advisors is equipped to handle them. Our main goal is to facilitate the right type of sale for your business which will best meet your needs and objectives.

How can sellers help expedite the sale of their business?

In a perfect world every business listed for sale would sell at a faster than average rate for exactly what price the seller was asking. We don't live in a perfect world though and this is part of the reason sales often take months or years and not days or weeks. Sellers can play a clear role in how quickly their business sells.

The best thing a seller looking for a quick sale can do is list their business at fair market value. This doesn't guarantee that a business will sell immediately, but it does make it much more likely because a buyer is looking to not overpay and to make sure the value of goods and services matches the asking price. Beyond this, if you start at a fair price, you may substantially reduce any time spent negotiating because the value of the business isn't only clear to you, it's also clear to anyone interested in purchasing it.

Another thing a seller can do to help expedite a sale is to offer seller financing. In this common scenario, the seller becomes the bank and finances a percentage of the deal. For example, as of 2024, Small Business Association (SBA) financing is at 11-15%. If the seller is willing to come in a little lower, such as between 7-8%, then it's for the benefit of all parties. Why? It's simple, the buyer of the business receives a more favorable deal, while as the seller you may receive tax benefits with regards to capital gains when not receiving the proceeds from the sale all at once since the financing will be spread out over time.

How sellers may accidentally prolong the sales process

In the same way that it's possible for a business owner to take certain steps to help expedite the sale of their business, it is also possible to make the process take longer than average. One of the biggest missteps is to insist that the assets are priced way over their market value. At Business Exit Advisors, we provide our clients with a range of what the business is most likely to sell for, and we are willing to list the business at the top tier of this range for the first 30-60 days. With that said, there are situations where this pricing needs to be reevaluated and to ensure that we're doing our due diligence, we meet with all of our clients on a regular basis. During these meetings, we look at factors like analytics (e.g. the amount of views and clicks on a business put up for sale through our online marketing) along with data about how it compares to other similar businesses on the market in terms of price and interest, the amount of Non-Disclosure Agreements (NDA) that have been signed, and any other general inquiries on the business. Combining all of this information allows us to make the necessary adjustments to ensure that your business sells in a timely manner and at a fair price. Remembering that we're on the same team and have the same goal of selling your business for what it's worth makes it easy to overcome the hurdle of insisting that your business must be listed above fair market value.

Exercises for Moving Forward

Selling a business does not have to be a complicated or a prolonged process provided you understand the basics of what it takes to make such a sale go as smoothly as possible. Thinking about what business brokers do, the steps of the business selling process, and how long the sale of a business may realistically take, please complete the following sentences, and use the answers you provide as a road map to help you navigate the rest of this process. Similar to the exercises found at the end of the last chapter some of these questions will be asked at later points in the book. As a reminder, it can be helpful to compare the answers provided in these earlier chapters with those provided in later chapters as a way of guiding you towards making the necessary decisions associated with the sale of your business.

1. In my own words I think the role of a business broker is to _____

_____.

2. I believe that a business broker fulfills their role when they _____

_____.

3. I think that the most important step of selling a business is _____

_____ because _____.

4. At the present time I think I am most prepared to address the _____

_____ (fill in the blank with one of the 7 steps of selling a business) step of selling a business because _____

_____.

5. At the present time I think I am least prepared to address the _____
_____ (fill in the blank with one of the 7 steps of selling
a business) step of selling a business because _____
_____.

6. Based on the preliminary work that I have done, and what I know about
how long the average sale time of a business the size of mine is, I think
that the sale of my business will take _____ months because
_____.

Selling a business is a process that requires leveraging knowledge
of not only what's allowable by law, but also what the market is willing to
bear. Based on this it can be a daunting task for some sellers. This doesn't
have to be the case for you though. At Business Exit Advisors, we're
transparent with you about what this process is, and we take on the stress
of selling your business, so you don't have to. We want you to be
knowledgeable and understand the value that the right business broker
brings to these types of transactions.

Now that you understand business selling basics, it's time to
conduct a preliminary business check-up.

3. BUSINESS CHECK-UP

"Even if you are on the right track, you'll get run over if you just sit there." - Will Rogers

Think of a business check-up as being akin to an annual check-up at your doctor's. The latter lets you know how healthy you are and what changes you may need to make to your lifestyle to live longer or improve your quality of life. Similarly, the former focuses on whether your business is fit to take to market as-is, and what your options realistically are if, for whatever reason, it isn't. What you may need to do during this check-up is going to vary widely based on the exact position that your business is in, and what may ultimately make it most attractive to potential buyers. All of this will be addressed on a case-by-case basis with Business Exit Advisors. With that said, there are some things that every business owner considering selling their business can and should do to assess how ready their business is to be sold.

Getting real about the reputation of your business

No matter how good you think your products or services are, what people are saying about your business is just as, if not more, important. The same is true for what people are saying about you, or the entity that owns your business. Why? Because, whether you like it or not, and whether it's fair or not, this is information that people, including potential buyers, are going to be judging the business on. Based on this, you need to be willing to check and address both the online and offline reputation of your company.

Checking and addressing the online reputation of the business

Chances are good that no matter what you sell or what services you provide your business will have some type of online presence. Based on what you do and how tech savvy you are, that presence can range from a profile on a single social media platform with only a few hundred followers to a dedicated website, several social media profiles, and extensive reviews. What matters at this juncture isn't the scope of your reach but instead what it looks like to someone who may be interested in buying your business. Based on this, there are several things that you need to be on the lookout for: what's being said, who's saying it, and how you've responded.

Assessing what's being said

Looking at what's being said about your business online is a self-explanatory task, you're simply looking for mentions of your business online. The clear starting place is on platforms you have some control over such as posts on social media profiles and testimonials on your website if they're available. From there branch out and look at any relevant reviews that have been left on third party sites. At this stage, try to be as objective as possible, especially if the information you're seeing is negative. Remember that you're not trying to control the narrative, and more importantly, it's not possible for you to do so. Instead, at this stage you just want to see what's being said about your business online, because that puts you in a position as that of an outsider assessing the reputation of your business for the first time.

Assessing who's saying what's being said

While the Internet can feel like a democracy in the sense that there seems to be space for everything and everyone, all comments don't hold equal weight. The reason for this is twofold. First, some comments are outright spam. Second, some comments have been posted with the specific purpose of discrediting you and/or your business.

Let's look at spam comments first. These comments are easy to spot because they usually contain the same or highly similar language regardless of where they're being posted. Any comments telling you to repost your content on a specific profile or site, comments offering financial payouts to new followers in exchange for a direct message. (Often containing a specific keyword or phrase), posts praising a financial or spiritual guru, and any posts that are obviously irrelevant can and should be ignored. Not only do these types of posts appear pretty much everywhere, but they're not the kind of posts that serious potential buyers are paying attention to.

What can be more detrimental than spam comments are negative comments that were posted with the specific intent of damaging your reputation or the reputation of your business. It's important not to immediately assume that these types of comments will count against you negatively, because they may not. For example, there are times when a business is flooded with negative reviews from people who have never used the product or services because of word-of-mouth, a news story, or in some cases because of jealous competitors. Taken at face value, these types of comments can seem incredibly damaging, but they don't have to be. If you can present potential buyers for your business with a rationale for why these comments may exist, they don't need to have an adverse impact on your reputation.

Assessing how you've responded

In many cases what is more important to your reputation than what's been said online about your business is how you or your team have chosen to respond to these comments. Businesses that respond promptly, courteously, and with potential solutions for any problems that have been presented may be deemed to be more friendly, reliable, and trustworthy than those who respond belatedly or not at all, as well as those where the responses are defensive or can be read as being argumentative. Similarly, if in the past you've only responded to one type of comment you may be perceived as not being thorough or not being realistic about how you approach your business, and this can scare some potential buyers away as they'll be inheriting this perception if they keep your business intact and operational as is.

Checking and addressing the offline reputation of the business

It's impossible for you to know absolutely everything that's being said about your business offline, but that's even more reason why you should be aware of information that you can check. Everything from magazine features to interviews on talk shows can, and do, influence the public perception of your business. More importantly, when you're looking to sell your business, this type of content can influence the perspective of prospective buyers as they consider what they do and do not want to be associated with. This assessment is identical to checking your online reputation so once again you need to be on the lookout for what's being said, who's saying it, and how you've responded.

Assessing what's being said

While you may have little to no control over what's being said about your business online, chances are good that you have been able to exert some influence over what's being said offline, even if only regarding consenting to certain interviews versus refusing others. Even with this being the case, when you're getting ready to sell your business it's a good time to double check what information is out there. If you don't have hard copies in your records, then look them up online to see if they've been archived. If they haven't been archived then for most people they don't currently exist, but you never know what someone may have seen in the past and committed to memory. Based on this it can be helpful to have a summary of what you remember appearing and where.

Assessing who's saying what's being said

Not all sources of information are equally respected or will be judged in the same way. While the quality and trustworthiness of the source plays some role in this so does perception. For example, if there's significant word of mouth about your business coming from various sources not connected directly to you and it's generally positive then this may ultimately hold more weight than one or two pieces of negative feedback in print. Keep in mind that it can be incredibly difficult to accurately gauge who is talking about your business offline because unless the information makes it to print you have no real way of tracking it. This doesn't mean that you shouldn't have an awareness of it. It does mean though that you may not always be able to accurately measure it.

Assessing how you've responded

Take a minute and think about the last time your business was praised or critiqued to your face, and how you reacted to that. Whether you realized it at the time or not your reaction in that moment could have had ramifications about the way that your business is looked at by others, especially if your response to the situation was memorable in some way for someone. Like assessing who is saying what about your business, it is almost impossible to accurately gauge how people are perceiving your responses. Thus, it is even more reason to ensure that your answers are even tempered and in line with the image that you want to present to the public.

Looking at current staff performance

If you plan on selling your business as a turn-key operation as opposed to selling off its assets, then you need to carefully consider the performance of all your current employees. Turn-key is a business that you can step into and operate and run immediately. Specifically, you need to take the time to engage in two key tasks: conducting performance reviews of every member of your staff and finding ways in which you can strengthen your workforce.

Conduct performance reviews

Based on the size and scope of your company you likely already conduct performance reviews of some kind even if only in an informal sense. When preparing to sell your business as a turn-key operation however it can be helpful to have up to date, formal performance reviews that can be shared with the new owner so that they have a snapshot of each employee along with their documented strengths, weaknesses, and their trajectory at the company. While such records do not serve as a guarantee that good employees will not be displaced in some way by whoever ultimately purchases your business, they do serve to offer clear reasons why they should not be.

Strengthen your workforce

Once performance reviews have been conducted, utilize the information that you've gleaned to strengthen your workforce; to make it as attractive to a potential buyer as possible. While doing this, you may be required to promote some workers while demoting others, as well as hiring new employees and firing those who are shown via their performance reviews not to be performing up to standard. These shifts help to ensure that the team of employees you have in place at the time of the sale is a team best equipped to handle the transition to new ownership because they are the most qualified, capable, and/or eager to learn and grow with the company.

Is your business aesthetically desirable to a buyer?

In real estate, it is not uncommon for renovations to a property to occur before it goes to market. These can range from minor changes like adding a fresh coat of paint to the outside of a building, to more significant ones like modernizing a part of the space. Taken at face value, these changes may seem like a waste of money, but the opposite can be true. Taking the time to update and upgrade before selling a property increases its value, and the same can be true when looking at selling your business. Based on this it is important to remember that looks matter and that making aesthetic changes can directly impact how your business is perceived when it goes to market.

Brick and mortar basics

If you run a brick-and-mortar business, then it's likely you already understand the importance of ensuring that your business is appealing to your clientele. It is also important to prospective buyers as well. This is true even if your business doesn't serve customers directly (such as a warehouse or manufacturing plant). In fact, businesses in these categories may have more work to do in terms of making updates and upgrades precisely because they do not cater to the general public. Aesthetically, there are two main areas that you'll want to focus on: the creation of curb appeal and addressing any issues inside the business. The rationale for this is simple: the more well maintained the business appears to be, the greater the faith a buyer may have in it from the outset.

Creating curb appeal

Succinctly defined, curb appeal refers to how nice a property looks on the outside. At the bare minimum, this should translate to a property being clean and free of hazards, having adequate lighting, and having the entrances and exits easily accessible. If this is not the case with your current business these are the areas to be addressed first.

Once your property meets the minimum standards for curb appeal you may think your work is done. It's not. You need to be mindful of two key things: the condition of any aesthetic elements that have become associated with the business and the possibility that some of these elements may suit your personal taste but don't align with industry standards.

In terms of the former, think about anything that possibly draws attention to your business. Maybe the building is painted an unusual color or has a large mural on the side, or perhaps it has become associated with some type of statuary that you have on the property. If these are things that your business is known for and associates with you, then you want to make sure that they are in the best condition possible.

In terms of the latter, think about the reality that aesthetic elements that may be appealing in some settings may be viewed as deterrents in others. For example, a water feature such as a large fountain may help create interest in a business like a boutique hotel but could be viewed as being an unnecessary expense for someone seeking to buy a business like a bottling plant where there is no need to directly appeal to customers.

Conversations with your business broker can help to narrow down precisely what it is that you should and shouldn't be focused on in terms of making your business aesthetically pleasing. When having these conversations, it's important to remember that Business Exit Advisor's goal is to help you present your business in its best light. In some instances, this may contradict with what you've done in the past or what you're doing in the present. Remember always that the goal is the future sale of your company.

Why what's inside counts

As important as it is to consider what the outside of your business looks like, it's equally important to ensure that the inside is appealing as well. There is no one-size-fits all formula for this because different types of businesses have different needs and things that are considered "must-have" in some industries are completely unimportant in others. For example, businesses like dance studios often have walls of mirrors, however this obviously isn't necessary, and could actually be a hazard in a large appliance store. Similarly, it's not uncommon for the floors of garages to be stained in some way, but it could possibly raise red flags about how well run a business is if the floors of a restaurant were stained in the same way. The takeaway from all of this is to carefully consider your business, what's standard for your industry, and what aesthetically raises red flags.

Assess your assets

If your business owns or leases any assets in addition to real estate, you will need to objectively assess it. Everything from machinery to company vehicles should be given a thorough once over to check if there are any pressing issues that need to be fixed or replaced before the sale of your business because all issues will need to be disclosed to potential buyers once your business is taken to market. Additionally, your intangible assets such as licensing agreements will need to be evaluated to make sure that they are in order and transferable to the new owner if they're integral to the day-to-day operations of your business and/or production of any products or the ability to render services.

A special note about website changes

Evaluating your website to possibly make changes may seem like a necessary step at the stage where you're conducting a business check-up. However, in addition to possibly being a waste of time, this may do more harm than good if it requires your website being down for any considerable length of time. The reason for this is directly related to how you're selling your business. If you're selling the assets only, the website may not matter at all to whoever ultimately buys your business because they won't need it or will only need it for a short period of time. Similarly, if you're selling the business as a turn-key operation it's probable that anyone who buys it is going to want to make some changes of their own, even if it's only to announce that the business is under new ownership.

Understanding exactly what you're selling

Selling a business does not look the same for everyone. Therefore, deciding exactly what will and will not be sold can have a potential impact on the sale by influencing not only who's interested but also what it is that they're willing to ultimately pay. When taking the time to figure this out there are a few considerations that you may want to make.

First, think about how the business is being sold. While having a clear accounting of what you're selling is important regardless of what type of sale it is, it may be especially important when the sale is being conducted under the auspice of an asset purchase agreement. The reasoning for this is simple: the more quality assets you must sell, the more interested potential buyers may be.

Next, consider what the new owner of the business will need to run it successfully as well as what may be a hindrance. For example, a photography studio without any photography equipment isn't really an attractive deal, and if all the equipment is outdated or in need of serious repairs the potential buyers may be equally leery about purchasing the business. As the seller, you need to not only think about these things but also communicate them to your broker so that they can package and position your business listing in the most appealing way possible without under delivering on seller expectations or over promising on your behalf.

Finally, you need to be able to articulate precisely what's valuable about your business to your broker so that they can communicate this to potential sellers. This is something that goes beyond placing dollar amounts on assets and instead needs to address the core of what it is that truly makes your business successful or special. For example, Business Exit Advisors had the pleasure of selling one of the largest produce companies in Florida to another large company. In this instance while the buyer added different elements to the business which resulted in them doubling the revenue of the company, they retained all the produce suppliers the previous company had. Retaining these suppliers wasn't something that they had to do under the terms of the sale, but it made sense to do so because these were established relationships that already existed between the companies that provided the produce and the company that had been purchased. Knowing that these relationships existed and being able to show their value led to a situation that not only benefited the buyer and the seller but also the end consumer. In contrast, Business Exit Advisors also had the pleasure of selling a huge pizza chain. While the fact that the sale went through was a success, the new owners changed everything from the employees to the recipes and negatively impacted the business. This immediate change is one that we advise against for at least the first 6 months so that the new owners have time to get acclimated to how the business runs as-is. As a seller, it's impossible to stop a buyer from doing something similar if they purchase your business, but they may be less inclined to do so if they have a clear understanding of why certain aspects of your business have an important value.

Cleaning up books and records

Anyone interested in buying your business will be allowed to have access to your financial books and records. However, there are a variety of legitimate reasons why you may be reluctant as a business owner to simply hand them over to a prospective buyer. Some reasons include not fully understanding what they contain yourself, a change in your accounting team, or the realization that they are not as up to date as they should be. Dealing with this can be both stressful and time consuming, and there's no universal way that business brokerages approach this issue.

Business Exit Advisors believes that you should be proactive about cleaning up your financial records before they are presented to buyers. Based on the scope and size of your business we can help you by bringing in a team of professionals who specialize in Business Forensic Accounting. This type of accounting can range from a small audit to a reclassification of the business entity. Additionally, we also work closely with your accountant to make sure there are no discrepancies and that everything aligns with the parameters of IRS filing practices over the years.

Exercises for Moving Forward

Conducting a business check-up largely means being willing to look at your business objectively, from the perspective of a potential buyer. This can be a difficult process, especially for business owners who have a significant amount of time or energy invested or for those who haven't previously considered the way that their business may be perceived or could be viewed. Additionally, it isn't always easy to make changes, even if they're needed. However, all of this is necessary when you're looking to sell your business. The following exercises are more in-depth than some of those presented in previous chapters and in some instances, require you to work with a professional in order to get the most accurate answers. This information can be used as foundational when working with a business brokerage. It will provide them with a snapshot of your business beyond your financial records.

1. Do an online search for your business. The first 3 results that are not your personal website or social media channels are for the following sites:

a. _____

b. _____

c. _____

If there are no sites that fit these criteria this is because _____, _____and skip exercise 4.

2. Review each of the 3 sites from the first exercise. What kind of sites are they e.g. personal blogs, review sites, news sites:

The first site is a _____ site.

The second site is a _____ site.

The third site is a _____site.

3. Based on the information found on the 3 sites the first 3 words that come to mind about my business are _____,
_____, and _____.

4. Ask someone else to do an online search for your business. The first 3 results that are not your personal website or social media channels that they found are for the following sites:

a. _____

b. _____

c. _____

5. Have the same individual from exercise 4 review each of the 3 sites from that exercise. What kind of sites are they e.g. personal blogs, review sites, news sites:

The first site is a _____ site.

The second site is a _____ site.

The third site is a _____site.

6. Based on the information found on the 3 sites ask the individual what are the first 3 words that come to mind about your business and record them here: _____, _____,
and _____.

7. The last time someone praised my business I _____
_____.

One result of this was _____

_____.

8. The last time someone criticized my business I _____

_____.

One result of this was _____

_____.

9. I think my business has a _____ reputation. The reason
why I think this is _____.

10. Ask 3 people about the reputation of your business and record their
responses here:

a. _____

_____.

b. _____

_____.

c. _____

_____.

11. *For those looking to sell turn-key operations only.*

The last time I conducted performance reviews on my employees was

_____. Based on these performance reviews I
made the following changes: _____

_____.

12. *For those looking to sell turn-key operations only.*

In conducting performance reviews before putting my business up for sale my goal is _____. I believe this will be best achieved by _____.

13. In order to increase curb appeal the following changes should ideally be made to my property:

_____

_____

_____

_____

If no changes need to be made its because _____

_____.

14. Ask 3 people about the changes that need to be made to improve the curb appeal of your business and record their responses here:

a. _____

_____.

b. _____

_____.

c. _____

_____.

15. To improve the inside of my business the following changes should ideally be made to my property:

_____

_____

_____

_____

If no changes need to be made its because _____

_____.

16. Ask 3 people about the changes that need to be made to improve the inside your business and record their responses here:

a. _____

_____

b. _____

_____

c. _____

_____

17. The top 3 most important assets my business has been: _____,

_____,and _____.

The asset in the best condition is _____

because_____.

The asset in the worst condition is _____

because_____.

Prior to taking my business to market I will address the asset in the worst condition currently by _____.

18. In selling my business what I am selling is _____

_____

_____.

I have decided on this because _____

_____ .

I would be willing to change my mind about what exactly is included in

the sale if _____ .

19. I would categorize my current books and records as _____

_____ . My reason

for this assertion is _____ .

Taking a truly objective look at your business offers you the ability to gain an in-depth understanding of what may and or may not make your company attractive to outsiders. When conducting this assessment, you shouldn't only be thinking about what potential buyers may be thinking, but also from the perspective of consumers and even competitors. This multifaceted focus allows you to consider both what's positive and what's negative so that you can be proactive when talking to us at Business Exit Advisors about ways to highlight the former and mitigate the latter.

Now that you have conducted a preliminary business check-up, you can start delving deeper into the process of what it takes to bring a business to market before the "For Sale" sign officially goes up.

BEFORE THE "FOR SALE"

Having completed the basics of looking at the size of your business, ownership, how it may be valued, its foundation to make a sale, and a "check-in", you may feel ready to go straight to market. However, we're not quite there yet. There are still some things that you need to consider before truly being ready to go through with the sales process.

This section will focus on what action needs to take place before you officially offer your business up for sale. When finished reading this section, you'll learn about the following topics:

- The nuances of a business valuation, including why it's important, how it may be conducted, the internal and external factors that may impact value, and how you can position your business for the best valuation.

- The legal considerations and documentation that you should keep in mind when preparing to sell a business.

- The reasons we are the right business broker to complete the sale of your business.

4. BUSINESS VALUATION

"Price is what you pay. Value is what you get." - Warren Buffet

The question of what your business is worth is one that has been asked before in this book, and it's perfectly okay if at this juncture you're still unsure. It's already been presented that the answer can be subjective based on who's being asked and to what they're assigning value. It's also been presented that there is an objective way to assess value. This will be handled by Business Exit Advisors who will utilize verifiable financial information, which is the same source that any reputable brokerage or appraiser will utilize. Though knowing this doesn't give you any insight into why this valuation is needed, how it may be completed, what can impact it, or how to position your business to receive the best valuation possible. For that information you'll need to keep reading.

Why a formal business valuation is needed

Many, if not all, business owners would probably prefer to be taken at their word when it comes to what their businesses are, or could potentially be, worth. If this were the case, there would be no need to undergo a formal business valuation and there would be one less step in the process of selling a business. This may seem like a solution that could streamline things; however, it would create more problems than it solved.

First, there is the very real issue that if business owners just set prices at will, the majority of what is offered for sale would only be available at prices that far exceed their actual worth. Without seeking to discount the work that people put into building a business in terms of both their capital and sweat equity, or all the intangible value that can be derived from things like the goodwill of the local community where a company is located, the reality is that many businesses would likely be grossly overvalued without utilizing formal metrics. Moreover, even if businesses were able to sell at inflated prices, the buyers may never make a return on their investment.

In contrast, there's also the possibility that some business owners may substantially undervalue their business. There are numerous ways in which this could feasibly happen, even to someone with a clear understanding of their market or industry, because other factors may be missed. While the eventual buyer would be getting a deal in the short term, in the long term it may lead to a similar mistake if the business is placed for sale again.

If you've ever seen an episode of "Shark Tank" or a similar show, or needed to pitch personally to investors, then you already understand how important an accurate valuation of your business is. Formal business valuations rely on data and formulas and it's for this reason that even when the results of different models show variations, they are still considered reliable. It's this reliability that helps to get businesses sold.

Business valuation basics

While you won't be responsible for determining the valuation of your business directly, it is important that you have a basic understanding of how a valuation is conducted. You should be aware of several key items including who is responsible for conducting business valuations, the two main types of valuations, and the fact that there are different valuation models used.

Who conducts a business valuation

Ideally, someone from outside the business should conduct the business valuation. As an outsider this individual is more likely to be objective when looking at your business and its overall value. Remember, what compensation you want for your business may not be what it's worth to someone looking to purchase it.

Understanding a Broker's Opinion of Value

A Broker's Opinion of Value (BOV) is a professional assessment of the estimated value of a property conducted by a business broker or an agent. In general, this estimate is derived from market research, comparable business sales, and the expertise of the broker. While this isn't a formal appraisal, and it may not be as detailed or precise as a certified appraisal conducted by a licensed appraiser, it's still highly useful because it can help not only buyers, but also sellers and investors get an idea of what the business may potentially be valued at in the current market. To conduct an initial appraisal, Business Exit Advisors utilizes a broader version of BOV by looking at the business for sale as a whole, as opposed to what physical property you may own. This appraisal, which includes all the components of a traditional BOV, provides us, and you, as the seller, with an idea of how the business may be more formally valued down the line, which in turn, helps us to best position it for sale.

Absolute valuation vs. relative valuation

Regardless of the specific valuation model utilized there are two types of valuation. These include absolute valuation and relative valuation. With absolute valuation, focus is placed solely on your business with consideration being given to dividends, cash flow, and the growth rate.

What this does is reveal the true value of the company by looking only at information that's directly relevant to it. In contrast, relative valuation models take a more expansive approach. Instead of focusing only on your business, they look at your business in relation to companies that are similar. Specifically, the models that use relative valuation, calculate various multiples and ratios, and compare them to the multiples of companies like yours.

Specific ways to calculate the value of a business

Looking at absolute valuation and relative valuation, what's being considered are broad ways business valuation can be approached. However, they do not represent the more nuanced methods that are actually used to undertake this task. Instead, there are numerous ways in which the value of a business is actually calculated. Some of these methods include calculating asset valuations, calculating liquidation value, utilizing the times revenue model, utilizing an earnings multiplier, or using the rule of thumb. While these represent some of the ways in which businesses can be valued, it is not a complete or comprehensive listing, and as such, it is entirely possible that when your business undergoes its own valuation, a different method may be used that is best suited to you and your company.

Asset valuations

When using asset valuations to assign value to the business as a whole, the current retail and wholesale value of all the assets a business owns are combined and totaled. This is a straightforward approach making it one of the easier ways to potentially value a business. Additionally, even without doing the exact math it is possible to get an idea of what the value of your business may be because companies that own high volume assets and/or a considerable amount of assets are likely going to have a higher valuation than those that have low value assets, and/or those that lease or license most of their assets.

Liquidation value

When using liquidation value as the litmus for business valuation what is considered is the value of all the assets held by the company if those assets need to be sold off in a limited amount of time (e.g. 12 months or less). While this approach is straightforward, it may be difficult to get a clear value as external factors can play a significant role in how items are priced during periods of liquidation. For example, consider the variance in discounts offered by stores going out of business. The percentage discount of items often gets steeper the longer that the liquidation goes on and so while stock may initially be priced at between 20% and 40% off, in the final days of a liquidation what remains may be priced at between 70% and 90% off. Noting this, such a valuation method may be best only if, as the owner of the business, you're willing to be extremely flexible about the possible sale price.

The times revenue model

The utilization of the times revenue model for business valuation requires assessing a stream of revenues that your business has generated over a specific period and then applying a multiplier. The exact multiplier is determined both by the industry your business is in and the overall economic environment. While this method can be one of the easier ones to calculate, especially in situations where a business has clear and complete records, it's also important to understand that it can be misleading. Potential valuations using this method may not be wholly accurate because it looks at revenue as opposed to profit, and while the two may rise in tandem, it's equally possible the former will increase while the latter remains the same or even declines based on the business and what it offers. For example, a product-based business may increase its prices based on an increase in the raw materials that it uses. This creates an increase in revenue but due to adjusted prices or other associated costs profit margins may not shift. As a result, the times revenue model may artificially inflate the value of a business.

Earnings multiplier

Calculating the value of a business utilizing an earnings multiplier is like making this calculation using the times revenue model. The key difference is that when using an earnings multiplier profits are used instead of revenue. Specifically, future profits are adjusted against cash flow that could be invested at the current interest rate over the same period. The result of this is the final figure generated is reflective of a more accurate view of what the business is worth since profits are a reliable indicator of the financial success that a company has achieved or may achieve in the future if they are sustained.

The rule of thumb

Conducting a business valuation using the rule of thumb can be one of the least reliable ways to value a business. This is since, in lieu of using financial information from the company, the selling prices of similar businesses are used to determine a probable future cash flow or annual gross revenue. This then determines the business valuation. While such a method is expeditious, it can also be wildly inaccurate because what a business is truly worth and what it ultimately sells for may be drastically different. For example, the owner of a company in a trendy industry may be able to command a price higher than the combined current value of the real property and associated IP, simply because a buyer wants to enter a market without facing barriers to entry. In contrast, the selling price of an established, asset-rich business may be low based on something unrelated such as the sudden financial hardship of the owner who is willing to sell the business at a lower price point in exchange for a quick payday. While the rule of thumb technically looks at averages there's nothing that says that the businesses selected can't be cherry picked which makes this particularly problematic as different individuals or companies using this same method can come to valuations that drastically differ from each other.

Business valuation with Business Exit Advisors

At Business Exit Advisors, the process of conducting a business valuation is completed individually for every business. While the specific steps can, and do, vary, the first steps are always the same. We initially review the available financial information and consider the physical assets of the business. Combined, this information is foundational to the process of providing a fair valuation.

The financial information that Business Exit Advisors requests includes 2-3 years of tax returns along with the most up to date profit and loss statement. In instances where this information isn't readily available, such as when dealing with smaller businesses, we will review information from sources such as QuickBooks. The purpose of collecting this financial data is simple; we want to start at the same place as most buyers who will be trying to understand how profitable the business is. Buyers want to see how much potential value they may ultimately derive from purchasing the business. By carefully looking over your financial information, we're able to assess where you're making money, where you're losing money, and what your seller discretionary earnings will be on an annual basis. You may already know exactly what these figures are, and it's great if you do, but any reputable business brokerage will want to double check and independently verify the numbers.

When looking at the physical assets that a business has this information can be provided in list form. However, that list should be as detailed as possible for the most accurate accounting. For example, if you own a used car dealership and the vehicles currently on your lot are going to be a part of the sale it may seem sufficient to simply include the make, model, and year of the car. This is good information, but what's even better is if you include known issues that might impact value. This is an extra step in the short term, but in the long term it can save time for everyone involved. Similarly, if a business is working out of a commercial space, we request information as to how much has been spent to date on tenant improvement, and what improvements may be needed to help the business be more salable. Finally, in instances where real estate is part of the transaction, we will need the most up to date appraisal for the property.

How valuation can be impacted

It would be remiss to think that the only factor that influences valuation is the financial well-being of your company. While that can, and does, play a significant role, there are additional aspects of your business and the broader market that need to be carefully considered as well. Some of these factors are internal, and therefore under your direct control, while others are external and may influence decisions, such as when or how you sell your business. In both cases being aware is important as it helps you to better understand why your business may be valued the way that it ultimately is.

Internal factors that can impact valuation

When looking at internal factors that can impact your valuation, focus should be placed on three key areas: your records, your assets, and how you run the business. All of these are items in your control. Knowing how they can help or hinder the valuation of your business allows you to adjust prior to taking your business to market.

The quality of record keeping

As a business owner your records are essential when you're looking to sell your company. Prospective buyers want to feel confident that they are investing their time and money in something worthwhile, and no matter how successful your business may be, red flags are raised when there isn't a clear paper trail that indicates why your business is successful. This is a large part of why taking the time to clean up your books and records is an integral part of conducting a business check-in as covered in the previous chapter.

When looking at the quality of your records there are two things to keep in mind: how complete they are and how consistent they are. Records that are incomplete or inconsistent can potentially reduce how your business is valued, based on where the gaps are and how large they are, as well as what discrepancies exist and why. Knowing this before your business goes to market gives you the opportunity to look over your records both individually and with your chosen business broker. This will ensure your business accounting is as accurate and complete as possible before it is shared with potential buyers.

As mentioned in the last chapter, Business Exit Advisors always take a proactive approach to addressing the books of our clients, also utilizing our external team that works both independently and with your accountant. This is not a service offered by all business brokers, and you may find yourself disappointed and in need of additional help if the brokerage you select doesn't offer these services, especially if you're currently uncertain about the quality of your record keeping.

The quality of your business assets

Whether you're leaning towards selling the assets associated with your business or selling your company as a turn-key operation, the quality of your assets is going to play a significant role. In the previous chapter you were advised to take the time to assess your assets, considering not only what they are, but also what condition they are in. Keep in mind that when looking at quality, newer does not automatically equal better, which is precisely why the focus is on the quality of your assets and not their age.

The quantity of your business assets

If you have an outright retail business, or a retail aspect of your business, and you're selling your assets or selling your company as a turn-key operation, the quantity of your assets is going to be important to consider. This is because not all inventory is necessarily valued the same way. Instead, for the purposes of business valuation, inventory can be separated into two distinct categories, sellable inventory, and non-salable inventory.

Sellable inventory consists of items that you have recently sold, and/or items that are likely to continue to sell after the business changes hands. These types of items add value to the sale of the business as whole.

For example, when Business Exit Advisors brokered the sale of a hardware store that had a significant amount of sellable inventory, we were able to increase the overall valuation of the business based on these assets.

In contrast to sellable inventory, there is non-salable inventory. These are items that have not recently sold and/or items that are not likely to sell once the business changes hands. While these items still count as assets because they do have some value even if they ultimately end up being sold for pennies on the dollar, they are unlikely to positively impact valuation even if there are a lot of them on hand at the time of the sale.

When looking at both salable and non-salable inventory, it's imperative from a valuation standpoint to have an accurate accounting of how much everything is worth. While you will likely already have some idea of this value which should be reported to your business broker, know that Business Exit Advisors will also do an independent inventory count. This will ensure the fairest deal for both you as the seller, and whoever ultimately buys your business. This will ensure that neither party is inadvertently shortchanged.

How your business assets are owned

How your business assets are owned can also play a critical role in the valuation of your business. The reasoning behind this is that when looking at your assets, items that are leased or licensed are weighed differently than items that are owned outright. For example, if you're looking to sell the assets associated with your business you may not be able to transfer leases of real property to the new owners and/or any intellectual property (IP) may be non-transferable as well. These considerations become even more important when you're looking to sell a turn-key operation because the potential inability to transfer some or all of your assets may decrease the value of your business.

How the business is run

When considering how the business is run for the purpose of valuation there are two key factors that are to be considered. The first factor is your Seller's Discretionary Earnings. The second factor is who is doing the work and how they're being paid. While these factors are being looked at separately, it's important to understand the relationship that they have to each other.

Seller's Discretionary Earnings factor into valuation because this number equates to the total financial benefit that a single full-time owner-operator derives from their business annually. Looking at this from a valuation perspective, this amount helps to provide potential buyers with an idea of what the return on their investment will be. The higher this number is, the higher the valuation that may be assigned to the business, and the more profitable the sale may ultimately be. While this seems straightforward, it can be complicated based on who is working for the business and in what capacity that work is being done.

Accurately calculating Seller's Discretionary Earnings can become difficult when looking at a sole proprietorship or family run business where all the work being done isn't necessarily being accounted for by the available financial records. For example, a small business owner may rely on a spouse or one of their children to design and maintain their website or to fill in when another employee calls out, and this individual may not be directly compensated. However, once the business is sold it will be necessary to replace this person, and that comes with a price tag which, depending on their exact role, may impact what the business is perceived to be worth. This is especially true in situations where there are key functions being performed that aren't being financially factored in as expenditures. Effectively, the more additional employees that may need to be hired to ensure the business runs at least as well as it does currently, the less money a potential buyer may be willing to pay, and the end-result is that it can adversely impact valuation. One way to mitigate this is to account for this before a final valuation is done. This will allow for a more realistic estimate.

External factors that can impact valuation

When looking at the external factors that can impact your business all prospective sellers need to consider several components. These factors include, The "Wawa Effect", the state of the overall economy, and current interest rates. While all good brokers will be aware of these issues, having some baseline knowledge puts you as the seller in a better position to understand the negotiations surrounding your business sale.

The "Wawa Effect"

The "Wawa Effect" isn't a formal business term. Instead, it refers to a phenomenon that has been observed by Business Exit Advisors regarding how a specific type of increased competition in a market can adversely impact the value of a business. Based on this, it's important to understand exactly what happened to the sale of gas stations once Wawa began to open more locations in the South Florida market, and how a similar situation could impact the sale of your business.

When gas stations are put up for sale, their valuation is based on how many gallons of gas they sell. Essentially, the more gallons of gas a gas station sells, the higher its' valuation. While this type of valuation is straightforward, it's also problematic for a seller if they see a sharp decrease in sales. This is precisely what happened to gas station owners in South Florida as Wawa extended its presence in the area. For other gas stations in the region, this posed an issue for three key reasons. First, Wawa can sell gas at a cheaper rate than some of its competitors. This may make it a more attractive option for someone looking to save money. Second, all Wawas have massive convenience stores in addition to gas pumps.. This can make them an attractive destination for someone who not only needs gas, but also needs to pick up something they forgot at the grocery store, lunch, or morning coffee. This is where the actual money is made in owning gas stations. Finally, Wawa is a part of a chain which may create a more consistent overall experience for customers. Business Exit Advisors saw the impact of this firsthand when we brokered the sale of a gas station following Wawa's expansion into the area. The valuation of the gas station significantly decreased along with the number of customers, and therefore gallons of gas.

Even if you aren't the current owner of a gas station you need to be aware of the "Wawa Effect". This is because almost every smaller business is at risk of having their valuation negatively impacted by the swift and sudden influx of large competitor in their area that quickly takes the market share. While Wawa has had this impact on gas stations, companies like Walmart and Target can pose similar threats to retailers in a variety of categories if they choose to enter, or significantly expand within a market. It's for this reason that Business Exit Advisors pays special attention to the movements of both direct and indirect competition whenever we're brokering a sale. This helps to ensure the sales take place at an optimal time to receive the best valuation.

Understanding the potential impact of the overall economy and interest rates

Every business owner is aware that the state of the economy and high interest rates can impact on their sales. What you may not be aware of is that these factors can also influence how your business is valued. Acknowledging this reality will help you to better understand why your business may receive different valuations based on different economic conditions.

The impact that the overall economy can have needs to be understood because this impacts what people are willing to invest in and purchase. Thus, the valuation of your business may change based on broader economic conditions.

Like shifts in the economy as a whole, changes in interest rates can also influence the valuation that a business ultimately receives. This can occur in one of two ways. First, when interest rates are on the rise, or deemed to be high, investors are looking to make investments they consider safe, and many businesses may simply not fit into that category. The result is a decreased demand for these businesses and as demand falls so does the value of the business. Second, with an increase in interest rates there is also an increase in uncertainty, and this may lead to investors demanding higher rates of return for the same amount of cash flow. In addition, the impact on cash flow of the business can also be negative because any debts can result in higher interest charges. Not only is this problematic for someone who is selling a business and may be carrying some debt that needs to be paid off before the sale goes through, but it can also be problematic from the perspective of a potential buyer who may be reluctant to take on any loans to finance the deal in whole or in part if they know they will be paying higher interest rates as a result of the transaction occurring at a time when interest rates are high versus waiting for the rates to be lowered.

It's important to understand that as a seller you're not completely at the mercy of the economy or rising interest rates, and that in fact you can potentially utilize these factors to your advantage in some circumstances. Business Exit Advisors has found that offering a buyer seller financing versus financing from a more traditional source, such as the local Small Business Administration (SBA), can lead to a mutually beneficial situation if as a seller you're willing to offer financing at a slightly lower rate than other lenders. First, by offering financing at a lower rate than the SBA or a bank, potential buyers may be more inclined to buy, which in turn keeps demand steady and stops the valuation of the business from dropping. Second, this also directly benefits you as a seller because you'll be responsible for lower capital gains taxes during the initial sale, and you'll receive a check every month the financing deal stays in place. In this scenario not only is your valuation unaffected, but you also legally decrease your tax burden. This isn't a solution that will work for all sellers or all businesses, but in scenarios where it may be viable, it is an option that is worth careful consideration.

Understanding the potential impact of market demand, current industry health, business location, and the reputation of your business: Special considerations for turn-key businesses

If you're interested in selling your business as a turn-key operation there are external factors in addition to the overall economy and interest rates that you must consider. Having an awareness of market demand associated with your products or services, knowing the current health of the industry, and being realistic about the location that your business is in, are all things you need to be prepared to focus on.

First, the existing market demand for a product or service should be easy to determine. However, similarly to the value that can be assigned to a business, there is a certain amount of subjectivity that may be at work when the owner of the company is the one presenting this information. In much the same way that many business owners believe that their business is worth top dollar, there is a desire to believe that there is sustainable market demand for what their business offers. In some cases, this is true and the market is relatively secure. In other cases, there is less surety about the stability or growth of market demand. In the latter instance the valuation assigned to the business may reflect this reality and be lower because of it.

Business Exit Advisors has found a way to potentially mitigate the issue of limited market demand by working with both sellers and buyers. For example, one of our previous clients was a buyer whose dream was to own a restaurant. To help ensure the likelihood that this would be sustainable for him, we took the time to research the area he wanted to open in and found that there was a demand for a good Chinese restaurant. This put the buyer in the position to purchase the space and assets he needed and use them as the launchpad to introduce a new restaurant concept into the area. It's important to understand that these types of deals can be positive for sellers as well. Unless you're looking to sell your business as a turn-key operation, the assets that make up your current business can be repurposed to create a new business for a buyer looking to enter the industry you're exiting to effectively limit the impact that fluctuating market demand can have on your valuation.

Next, when assessing market demand for your product or service, you're looking specifically at your business and what's being offered while having direct access to your financial records. This is not the case when assessing the current health of the industry that your business is in. To develop an idea about how healthy an industry is, you need to be able to objectively look at how businesses similar to yours, are faring. Thus, you will need to do research to find a way to sift between what's factual and important versus what's conjecture and can largely be ignored. You will find that having a business in an industry that is considered a good investment based on its stability or growth trajectory may have a positive impact while a business in a volatile industry or one whose growth is stagnant, or trending downward may have a negative impact on the valuation of your business.

One industry where Business Exit Advisors has seen low and declining valuations is in the retail sector. Both standalone stores and shopping malls have been negatively impacted by e-commerce giants like Amazon that offer a one-stop shopping experience that people can access from almost anywhere along with perks like lower costs and free shipping. These things make competition difficult. Two exceptions to this are retailers that sell niche or hard to find items and those who have made their stores destinations by offering and hosting consistent events. As a seller, you need to be aware of this reality so that you can be prepared for a valuation that may be lower than expected if you're in retail or an industry that has been or is on the verge of being similarly impacted.

Next, when you're selling a turn-key operation that operates out of a brick-and-mortar location (versus e-commerce), where the business is physically located can also play a significant role in business valuation. It would be remiss to assume that being in what's considered a "good" neighborhood will automatically equal a higher possible valuation while being located in what's considered a "less than desirable" neighborhood will automatically equal a lower possible valuation. There are numerous reasons why it isn't so simple. For example, nicer locations may mean higher property taxes that would ultimately fall to the buyer to pay. Similarly, a location that currently isn't one where many people have businesses simply be in a transitional phase and thus maintaining a presence there could lead to positive incentives down the line. These factors will be considered when the valuation of your business is completed.

One way to mitigate the impact that the location may have on the business is to have the sale structured in such a way that the purchase of the company is separated from where it's located. If you don't own the real estate associated with your business this will be necessary anyway. However, if you do own real estate, you should carefully consider if it makes more sense to sell the entities separately. For example, Business Exit Advisors worked with a seller who owned an oceanfront gift shop in South Florida. Not only was the business doing well, but the location was also beautiful. With this combination the sales should have been all but guaranteed to go quickly. What made finding a buyer tricky though was the financial responsibilities associated with where the business was located. In addition to the taxes, there was a need for flood insurance which the new owners would be required to purchase. Business Exit Advisors worked with the seller to sell the real estate to one buyer and the business assets to another buyer. The new business buyer was then able to move the business across the street to an area that still had ocean views but was less expensive to maintain.

Finally, while the reputation of a business is not quantifiable in terms of dollars and cents and isn't included in formal valuation models, it can, in some instances, add or detract from the value of the business. For example, businesses that have positive reputations oftentimes have profits to match. This is because they become go-to locations based on factors like quality products, reliable services, or the knowledge or positive attitudes of the staff. In contrast, businesses with substandard reputations may have inconsistent or declining profits especially as word about them spreads.

Positioning your business for the best valuation

To position your business to receive the best possible valuation the most important thing that you can do is plan. Business Exit Advisors advises all clients to prepare early and to handle preparations strategically. This is important whether you're looking to sell your business ASAP or if you have your sights set on selling in the future.

When working with a seller, Business Exit Advisors utilizes a complete team including an analyst, a financial advisor, and a professional well versed in both marketing and sales of your business. Together with the business owner we address the business not only as an individual entity but also as a part of the broader industry in which they operate and the market at large. Using this research, we can then present you with a valuation range. While there are sale price factors that will impact the exact number ultimately received, one of the things to keep in mind is that the more quickly you want the business to sell, the less money you may realize from the sale.

Exercises for Moving Forward

Making determinations about how a business should be valued is not a one-size-fits-all process, nor is it one that occurs in a vacuum. Unknown valuation may make this part of the process one of the more difficult aspects of preparing to take a business to market. To ease some of the tension that may surround it, it can be helpful to be as organized as possible in advance of taking your business to market.

1. I *perceive* the value of my business to be _____ (fill in the blank with the dollar amount). My basis for this valuation is _____ _____.

The *potential* value for this business within the next year is _____ (fill in the blank with the dollar amount). My basis for this valuation is _____.

The current *real* value of my business based on its total assets minus its total liabilities is _____ (fill in the blank with the dollar amount).

2. Ideally, I'd like to receive _____ (fill in the blank with the dollar amount) for my business. I think that this amount is a reasonable asking price because _____.

3. Of the various methods and models for business valuation discussed in this chapter I believe the following would provide the most favorable outcome for my business: _____. My rationale for this is _____ _____.

4. Of the various methods and models for business valuation discussed in this chapter I believe the following would provide the most least outcome for my business: _____. My rationale for this is _____
_____.

5. I think that the internal factor that is most likely to positively impact my business valuation is _____
because_____.

6. I think that the internal factor that is most likely to negatively impact my business valuation is _____
because _____.
I can potentially mitigate this impact by _____
_____.

7. Looking at the *quality* of my business assets, the most valuable asset my business owns is _____.
The current real value of this asset is _____ (fill in the blank with the dollar amount).

8. Looking at the *quantity* of my business assets my business has
_____ (insert amount) tangible business assets.

If your business has inventory that will be a part of the sale, answer the following question. If your business does not have inventory, or if the inventory you have will not be included in the sale, skip exercise 10.

9. On hand my business has _____ (insert amount) pieces of inventory. Of this inventory _____ (insert amount) of the pieces are sellable inventory, and their combined value is _____ (insert dollar amount). Of this inventory _____ (insert amount) of pieces are non-sellable inventory, and their combined value is _____ (insert dollar amount).

10. I think that the external factor that is most likely to positively impact my business valuation is _____ because_____.

11. I think that the external factor that is most likely to negatively impact my business valuation is _____ because _____. I can potentially mitigate this impact by _____

_____.

12. I think that in order to position my business for the best valuation the first thing I need to do is _____. This step is necessary because _____.

While business valuation is, at its core, a subjective process, it's a key step in the process of selling your business. Understanding that different valuation methods may yield different results, and that shifting internal and external conditions can influence valuation helps sellers to work with their brokers. In turn, this allows all parties to make the best decisions about how much a business can realistically sell for, and when it may be best to put it on the market.

Now that you know what goes into completing a business valuation, focus can be placed on the legal considerations you need to make before you put your business up for sale.

5. LET'S GET LEGAL

"Business owners should not have to choose between violating their faith and violating the law." – David Green

Legal matters are commonplace for all business owners. There's a need to be aware of things like what taxes you owe, or what licenses or permits you need, and it is ultimately your responsibility to ensure that you're in compliance. Based on this, it should be no surprise that the process of selling a business requires some focus on the law. This goes beyond whether you're legally allowed to sell the business, and instead focuses on factors that may hinder the sale in some way if they aren't adequately addressed and rectified. Business Exit Advisors works closely with in-house counsel to assess any potential legal issues, to be best prepared for the impact they may have. Taking the time to do this before your business is put up for sale helps to best protect your interests and those of any potential sellers so as not to ignore anything that may cause legal trouble later. Ideally, this process is just an exercise in being cautious, but in situations when it's necessary, this step can save you money even when it takes more time than you initially anticipated.

Potential legal red flags for a prospective buyer

Take a minute and think about your business in terms of what you sell or what services you offer, and how those sales or services are facilitated. If you weren't already the owner of your business, is there anything about any aspect about what you do that would potentially stand out as being problematic? If those issues are illegal in any way, they might signal a potential red flag for prospective buyers and that could stop a sale before it even starts. The most immediate issues in this regard may center around contestable intellectual property (IP) as in IP that can't be legally protected, unproven technology, or litigation involving your business. While these are some of the more commonplace issues, it's important to note that they're not the only ones that may signal potential trouble. Any brokerage doing its due diligence in working to sell your business will be sure to consider any special issues that may be unique to your company or your situation to help you resolve them.

Contestable IP

First, focus should be placed on whether your business relies in some way on contestable IP that will ultimately be a part of the sale. This type of IP can include, but may not be limited to, the logo for your business, a mascot, or proprietary software. What makes IP contestable can vary but essentially, it's anything that may potentially be viewed as infringing on an existing trademark or copyright even if no lawsuits have been brought against you or your company. While it is likely that you have already consulted with a lawyer or otherwise did your due diligence regarding IP to ensure that there would not be any issues in the future, it never hurts to double-check to make sure that it holds up under legal scrutiny. Taking the time to scrutinize any potentially problematic IP can be especially important for businesses that didn't develop some or all of their IP in-house, or did so without checking to ensure whether or not elements, such as the chosen font was commercial user friendly, or that any images, audio or incorporated video were properly licensed, and used within the parameters of that licensing, or freely available in the public domain.

Ideally, you know for a fact, and have all the necessary documentation to prove that your IP is above reproach. If this is the case it doesn't mean it'll never be questioned, but it does make it highly likely that any future claims will be decided in your favor. If this isn't the case then you need to determine what issues may exist, and how they can be rectified. Working one-on-one with a lawyer, or with a brokerage like Business Exit Advisors that has attorneys on staff, can, and will, make figuring out how to best prove the originality of your IP a much easier task than if you were to undertake it on your own.

IP that can't be legally protected

Second, from the perspective of a potential buyer what may be even more problematic than contestable IP is IP that can't be legally protected and therefore can't or shouldn't be used. It's remiss to think that just because you had IP personally created for your business that it's legally protected, because this isn't always the case. Specifically, there are three main reasons why your IP may not be able to be legally protected. These instances include IP that has been found to rightfully belong to someone else, IP that uses something freely available in the public domain without altering it, and IP that was created by artificial intelligence (AI).

One of the reasons buyers may be leery about buying a business where the associated IP is contestable, is that there is a real possibility that the IP in question may be found to rightfully belong to someone else. In instances where it's found that the IP doesn't belong to a business that's using it, there are a lot of potential legal consequences, one of which is that the business that was found to be using it illegally can no longer utilize it without violating the law. For well-established businesses this can be highly detrimental, especially if the potential seller was hoping to capitalize off the reputation of the previous business and its' IP.

It is important to note that just because some IP can't be legally protected doesn't mean that it can't be legally used. This is true in the case of IP that utilizes something from the public domain as-is and/or for IP that was created by AI. Potential buyers may be concerned if any of your IP falls into one, or both, of these two categories.

In terms of the former, there are instances in which businesses have been built, and more importantly thrive by creating IP based on something available in the public domain. One of the best examples of this is Disney, as many of its princess stories are based on fairytales that have been in the public domain for centuries. Disney's IP is protected though, because they didn't use those stories word for word and instead created their own narratives which they then applied for, and received, copyright protection. Therefore, while the original stories can be used by anyone, and cannot be legally protected, the IP that Disney created from them is legally protected. If the IP for your business uses something from the public domain that has not been altered, then any other business is welcome to use it as well. Potential buyers may be concerned about the negative ways in which this could impact the business in the future, even if it isn't a problem that you currently face.

In terms of IP created by AI, focus should be placed on generative AI. With the rise of this specific technology, it's important to note that as of the publication of this book, work that has been solely created using this technology is not legally protected. What this means is that if any of the IP created for your business was created using generative AI, you may not be able to stop other people from using it. If you, as the current business owner, don't have the ability to stop the IP from being used by others, then potential buyers may not be willing to try and fight for it either.

If you realize that you have IP that can't be legally protected, don't immediately panic as it may be possible to put protections in place. Instead, take the time to discuss this information with your lawyer and your business broker. You may be able to find a solution that allows for the IP in question to be both protected and therefore included as a part of your overall business evaluation and the eventual sale.

Unproven technology

Next, focus on the problems that may be associated with unproven technology. While it's completely possible that your business is the home of something like the next ChatGPT, prospective buyers will also want to be assured that it's not the next Theranos. That becomes more difficult in instances where your assets include unproven technology. Some buyers may have no problem taking a risk on a company whose value proposition is reliant on technology that's new or hasn't yet been fully tested, because they're interested in the potential long-term reward if it is actually revolutionary. However, for some buyers this will be too big a gamble for them to take and as such, their continued interest may be contingent on things such as your acceptance of a lower price.

The easiest way to mitigate any fears that potential buyers may have about the viability of your technology may be to demonstrate that it works. Prior to conducting any demonstrations though make sure that you've taken the necessary steps to protect your IP and that, if applicable, any buyers who are interested have signed non-disclosure and/or non-compete agreements.

Litigation

While businesses that are in legal trouble may be available for sale at lower rates than businesses without these troubles, the average buyer isn't interested in a low-price tag if it comes with too many complications. Possible litigation, ongoing litigation, and recently concluded litigation all present potential buyers with a unique set of threats. As a seller you need to be prepared to navigate if this reflects a position that you're in.

Possible litigation

If there is anything about your business or your business practices that may open you up to being sued, this can have a negative impact on the sale of your business. Thus, even if the plan is for the original company to be dissolved, such as a sale via an asset purchase agreement, it's still possible for the new owner to feel as if they will inherit the stigma associated with the situation. This is especially true in cases where the business is retaining its original name as a part of the sale or if the business is going to remain in the same location. Under such circumstances the new owners may be concerned about their ability to fully recoup their investment, or they may worry they will be directly associated with the litigated issue even though they had nothing to do with it. Additionally, even if the claims are frivolous or completely without merit, the threat of a business being faced with legal action can rightfully make buyers question if they want to buy a company navigating potential legal problems.

While it's impossible to predict whether you or your business will ever be sued, there are some indicators that may display a probable scenario. One indicator, contestable IP, has already been discussed. There are also other possible indicators, such as disgruntled former or current suppliers, partners, or employees, poorly executed contracts, or active disputes regarding things like licensing or leasing agreements. These issues would also be a red flag to prospective buyers. If your lawyer is aware that these issues exist, it is likely that they are advising you how to best address them. However, if you do not have counsel or if they are not aware of these problems, then it may fall to your business broker to help you to ensure that your business gets the best valuation. This is one of the areas where Business Exit Advisors in house council can come into play.

Ongoing litigation

It's entirely legal for a business to be sold during a lawsuit, but these types of sales come with caveats that as the buyer you need to be aware. Obviously, ongoing litigation can be damaging to a business in a variety of ways including negatively impacting sales, decreasing the valuation of the company, and changing the way the company is perceived. It's important to understand that even if you or the business is found to be blameless, the adverse impacts may not be immediately reversed. There are some buyers who will try to use this to their advantage by attempting to negotiate a much lower price regardless of how well the company performed before the litigation began. It's important to note that ongoing litigation does not mean you need to accept less than you want for your business.

While you should always strive to have the best team on your side when you're selling a business, it's critical in a situation where you need to sell your business while during a lawsuit. The best brokerage in this situation is Business Exit Advisors, because we have attorneys on staff and therefore have more consistent access to legal resources than a brokerage that outsources client legal issues to outside firms.

Recently concluded litigation

Recently concluded litigation may seem like a strange thing for prospective buyers to potentially be concerned about, but this is especially true in situations where the lawsuit was found in favor of the business owner, or the business being sold. Think about it another way; recent involvement in legal proceedings can mean recent damage to the reputation of the business. Based on the volume of press coverage, the specific allegations that were levied, and how the matter played out in the court of public opinion, buyers may be reluctant to become attached to a company. This is especially true if the new owner will be reliant on the IP of the business, its name, its location, or anything that may have even been tangentially associated with the lawsuit. The matter becomes one that's even more complicated if the business owner or business was found to be at fault and now has financial or social obligations to be met because of the ruling.

As well seasoned business brokerages, such as Business Exit Advisors, will be able to best position your business in the market following recently concluded litigation. The specific plan of action will vary based on the exact circumstances. In such a situation, it's important to be flexible and to understand that there may be differences between the way in which you would ideally position your business for sale and the way in which it ultimately needs to be positioned, to get you the best offer.

The documentation every business needs

Efficient and effective legal work is dependent on a large part on accurate paperwork. Regardless of how a business is owned, its size, or what industry it operates in, there is some documentation that all business owners need to have completed and readily accessible in preparation for selling their business. These documents include shareholder or operating agreements, up to date financial records, real property leases, other contracts, and documentation of IP ownership. These documents are ones that all businesses should have simply as a matter of protecting themselves legally, and they will all play a role in the sale.

Shareholders agreements or operating agreements

As the owner of an established business, you should already have shareholder agreements or operating agreements in place. However, you may not necessarily refer to these documents in this way. This can be especially true for owners of small businesses or sole proprietors. These are effectively any written agreements that you have, relating to the ownership of the business.

The importance of these documents is that they show the legal owner of the business and your right to sell it. Additionally, these documents indicate if anyone else has a legitimate claim to the business or any of its assets. Without proper documentation a business brokerage may be unwilling or unable to work with you until or unless you can prove that you can legally sell the business.

Up-to-date financial records

The importance of up-to-date financial records has been previously discussed in an earlier chapter; however, their value is worth reiterating. The ability to clearly prove both assets and liabilities or debts of a business is certainly something that a seller will be interested in. This information can also help you as a buyer by supporting a more robust valuation of your business, especially if the numbers indicate that you have been profitable.

Business Exit Advisors understands that while these documents are critical, they are not always maintained in a way that reflects profitability. It is for this reason that we work with business owners to help them clean up their books and records. This helps to ensure that the most accurate accounting for the business is presented and that there are no discrepancies between the various financial accounts that may exist.

Real property leases and other contracts

If you rent, own, or lease any type of property for your business you should have documentation that asserts this. Unfortunately, this documentation isn't always up to date and as such is open to potential contest later, such as when you're ready to sell your business. Similarly, based on your business, there are various other contracts that are consistently in play including, but not limited to, licensing agreements, employee contracts, and agreements with suppliers, vendors, or other outlets.

While these agreements are an important aspect of any sale, they are especially important in situations where the sale is going to be an asset purchase agreement. The reason for this is that they help to clearly show which assets the business owns outright and can therefore be counted as a part of the valuation, and which assets are rented, leased, or licensed, which may necessitate the new owner renegotiating terms which may require them to pay a higher rate.

Documentation of IP ownership

The IP owned by a company can represent some of its most valuable assets. However, that value is all but null and void if a business can't prove that the IP truly belongs to them and is protected. It's for this reason that all IP ownership needs to be carefully documented to show not only who owns the IP but also how it can be legally used.

Ideally, as the owner of the business, especially in situations where someone is looking to sell a turn-key operation, there must be clear and verifiable records pertaining to things such as the design of the logo, trademarks and patents held by the company, and any other form of IP. If this isn't the case, based on what the IP is and when it was created, it may be difficult to get documentation. This is an issue that can be further exacerbated if work on the IP was outsourced to freelancers who the business owner is no longer in contract with or contracted with or had contracted with a company that's now defunct. A brokerage like Business Exit Advisors will work diligently with you to ensure that all IP that can be legally protected is also clearly documented.

Corporation considerations

If you are the owner of a corporation, then in addition to the above documentation, there is an additional consideration to keep in mind. Specifically, you need to be sure that you have an up-to-date corporate Minute Book. The rationale for this is that the Minute Book contains records of your corporate actions, and as such, it may be requested for review as a part of the sales process.

It is likely that you already have an up-to-date Minute Book for your corporation, but there may be reasons why you do not. If this is the case for your business, and you cannot produce this documentation, this needs to be immediately discussed with your selected business brokerage. Business Exit Advisors understands how critical this documentation is for a corporation and we'll work with you as the owner to help ensure that these files are as complete as possible in full compliance with the law.

Turn-key sale considerations

If you're the owner of a business who is looking to sell a turn-key operation, then in addition to all the documentation required by all business owners, there are also several other types of documents that you need to have readily accessible. These documents include up to date human resource records, up to date information regarding employee benefit plans, and, if applicable, an employee agreement. The importance of these documents cannot be overstated as they will help to ensure that your business runs smoothly even when you are no longer its' owner.

Up to date Human Resource records

Human Resource records can provide a window into a company that may otherwise not exist because they document employee behavior. For potential buyers of turnkey businesses, these records can help them get an objective perspective of the individuals who will be working for them by providing information on how they have performed in the past and what interpersonal relationships may exist between different members of the staff. While such records do not serve, and should not be used, to replace in-person observations on the part of potential buyers and the eventual new owner, they are crucial supplementary material, because they help to reveal employee growth potential, or employee challenges by offering information that spans a period that may exceed the time that is allotted for observation.

While Human Resource records should be updated in real time to be as accurate as possible, there are some instances in which these records may need to be refreshed. This is one reason why as a part of your business check-up, Business Exit Advisors advocates for owners looking to sell turn-key operations to conduct performance reviews. In addition to being key in helping to assess the strengths and weaknesses of employees and to adjust as necessary, these reviews also help to ensure that there is recent information available for all employees who are currently working for you, and who may ultimately end up working for the new owner.

Up-to-date employee benefit plans

One of the key reasons that a business owner may choose to sell their business as a turn-key operation is to decrease the likelihood that their current employees will need to find new employment once the business is sold. This kind of employee-centered thinking does offer employees some potential protection. However, it does not mean that the employees will have the same protections and benefits that they did while you owned the business. It's for this reason that having up to date employee benefit plans available for review by potential buyers is important.

Even when selling a business as a turn-key operation, the new seller isn't inherently obligated to keep your existing employee benefit plans in place. However, if keeping these plans is a priority for you, then this is something that should be discussed upfront with your selected business brokerage. Having this discussion early may allow for additions to the purchase agreement, such as one which specifies that existing employee benefits must remain unchanged for a specific period of time. However, it is important to note that it may not even be necessary for such an addition to be made. If your business is successful and profitable with the current employee benefits in place, potential buyers may not wish to replace, update, or otherwise change them because they have been proven not to be a liability based on the way the business currently operates.

Employment agreements

Despite what it is called, an employee agreement in this context does not refer to agreements between the existing business and its employees. Instead, it refers to an agreement that can be drafted between the buyer and seller. Based on this, all turn-key businesses will not require an employee agreement to be put into place, but it will be necessary if the buyer wants you to remain involved in the business during a specified transition period and you agree to this arrangement.

Business Exit Advisors works closely with buyers and sellers to draft these types of contracts. By working with both parties on this document it helps to ensure that the final agreement has fair terms for everyone involved.

Necessary documentation for the sales process

The process of selling a business generates documents in addition to those that you should already have. In general, these documents may include non-disclosure agreements, non-compete agreements, the letter of intent, and contracts for the sale of the business. Additionally, based on the type of sale, your chosen business brokerage may find it necessary to draw up additional contracts and agreements, including one that outlines the relationship between you and them.

Non-Disclosure Agreements

Based on the nature of your business, you may not be familiar with the purpose or role of a non-disclosure agreement. Briefly presented, where allowable by law, these agreements prevent individuals from discussing certain business information, financial and otherwise. It's advisable when selling a business that these agreements are executed between the seller and potential buyers.

Within the context of a business sale, non-disclosure agreements require everyone involved in the sale to keep every aspect of the transaction confidential. This provides legal protection to the seller who may need to disclose information that isn't publicly available to potential buyers by preventing those interested in the business from sharing that information with third parties. Even in instances where it may not immediately seem necessary for a non-disclosure agreement to be put in place, Business Exit Advisors can provide this documentation as a means of legally protecting the seller.

Non-compete agreements

Like non-disclosure agreements, non-compete agreements may not be familiar to all business owners. Effectively these types of agreements, where allowable by law, serve to prevent competition in a specific area and/or for a specific amount of time. When selling a business, the buyer may request that in exchange for being paid a specific amount, which may be a portion of the sales price, that the seller will not set themselves up as competition to the buyer of their business by opening a business that is similar in nature once the sale is complete. Non-compete agreements may also be tailored with specific stipulations that can govern additional seller actions, such as disallowing them from utilizing their existing customer lists or the trade secrets from the business that they are selling.

It is also important to note that standard non-compete agreements are only enforceable for a certain amount of time versus in perpetuity and that they only cover a specific area. What this means is that if you decide at a later point you would like to start a similar business to the one you sold, then you are free to do so once the time on the non-compete agreement runs out.

Letter of Intent

When selling a business, a Letter of Intent (LOI) isn't a document that you'll initially have but instead one that you'll receive. An LOI is received from a potential buyer, and it declares their desire to purchase the business. Additionally, this document will indicate a suggested purchase price for the business, a timeline for the sale, and lay out any pertinent legal and procedural information. Effectively, the role of an LOI is to try to save time and costs by acting as the basis for the final purchase agreement.

It's important to understand that an LOI isn't legally binding and as a seller who receives the document, you're under no obligation to accept the terms that it outlines if you don't find them agreeable. However, agreeable terms are only one small part of the process. Once an LOI is received and agreed upon by a seller, Business Exit Advisors performs our due diligence by making sure that the business will be ready to sell within the prospective buyer's time frame and ensures that the buyer is qualified. Additionally, if the situation warrants it, we work with sellers to determine if additional negotiation is necessary or if the LOI should be treated as the next logical step in the context of the specific sale process.

Contracts for the sale of the business

At the conclusion of the sale of any business the most important document is the contract that outlines the terms of the sale. At minimum this documentation includes the purchase sale agreement but can also include other documentation related to the sale of the business.

Purchase sale agreements can vary based on the specific sale, however there are standard elements that all these contracts include. In addition to listing the involved parties, these agreements also include information about the exact assets that are being transferred or sold, any liabilities that the buyer will ultimately be responsible for, the terms of the sale, and any necessary disclosures. Effectively, this agreement specifies who the buyer and seller are, what the buyer is receiving as a part of the purchase, and what liabilities the buyer has incurred as a part of the purchase. This document will also include as caveat stating that the buyer will not be responsible for items that may include liabilities explicitly listed, sale price, the sale term, sale timeline, and any potential factors that may hinder the deal from moving forward as outlined.

In addition to the purchase sale agreement, documents such as non-disclosure agreements and non-compete agreements may also be included as a part of the contracts for the sale of the business. Based on the terms of the business sale, your business broker may also decide to include other documents such as those that outline how any disputes between the buyer and seller will be resolved. At Business Exit Advisors, we understand that business sales are not one-size-fits-all and as such, we tailor the contracts for the sale of the business to reflect the needs of the buyer and seller as they present themselves within the context of each individual sale.

Additional documents that Business Exit Advisors requires

Not all business brokers or business brokerages require the same documents when brokering a sale. In addition to the documents presented above, Business Exit Advisors also includes financial affidavits. The purpose of a financial affidavit is to vet all potential buyers. This document is a sworn statement signed after the buyer is vetted which indicates that they have the means to follow through with the purchase of the sale. Not all brokers will request the completion of this affidavit, but we know that it offers all our sellers an extra layer of protection.

Exercises for Moving Forward

While all qualified business brokerages will perform due diligence to ensure there are no legal issues to hinder the potential sale of a business, this process is one that can be streamlined by conscientious business owners. By taking the time to objectively look at your business from a legal standpoint, you put yourself and your brokers in the most advantageous position to either address existing issues or to help ensure that new issues do not arise before the business is put on the market.

If you think that your business has potential legal red flags go to question 1. However, if you do not think that your business has any potential red flags, skip directly to exercise 3.

1. Looking at my business a potential legal red flag that needs to be addressed is _____.
This issue exists because _____.
In the past I have tried to fix this issue by _____
_____ OR I have avoided addressing this issue in the past because _____
_____.
I will present this issue to a business broker by _____
_____.

2. If this legal red flag impacts the valuation of my business, I am willing to lower my asking price to _____ (insert a dollar amount). The lowest offer I am willing to accept based on this issue is _____ (insert dollar amount). I believe that this price is fair because _____
_____.

3. Noting that there are no potential legal red flags associated with my business I plan to maintain this positive status quo by _____
_____.

4. Looking at the required documentation for all businesses, the documentation that I feel is my business *strongest* is _____. My reason for this assessment is
_____
_____.

5. Looking at the required documentation for all businesses, the documentation that I feel is my business *weakest* is
_____. My reason for this assessment is
_____
_____.

I hope that a business broker can help me address this weakness prior to putting my business up for sale by _____
_____.

If any of the specified required documents are missing, answer question 6. If none of the documents are missing proceed to exercise 7.

6. The required documentation that I'm missing is _____.
I am missing this documentation because _____
_____.

Instead of this documentation I have _____
_____. The most important part of this
alternative documentation is _____
because _____.
I think that this will be helpful to share with a business broker because
_____.

7. Looking at the *quality* of my existing documents I would rate the
overall quality as a _____ out of 10. My reason for this rating is
_____
_____.

Legal considerations surrounding the sale of a business can be a complex matter. However, with the right business brokerage by your side this part of the process does not have to be difficult to navigate. Instead, our team at Business Exit Advisors can, and will, easily integrate attorneys into the business selling process to ensure that you are as legally protected as possible.

Now that you have an idea of the legal aspects that can be associated with selling a business, focus can be placed on the process of finding the right business broker. While Business Exit Advisors hopes to earn your trust and by extension your business, one of our top priorities is to ensure that all buyers and sellers work with a business brokerage that is best suited to meeting their specific needs.

6. FINDING THE RIGHT BUSINESS BROKER

"Example isn't another way to teach, it is the only way to teach."
- Albert Einstein

There's a crucial difference between finding a good broker to facilitate the sale of your business and the right business broker to take your company to market. There are a lot of good business brokers, individuals, and brokerages that are not only competent but also have had significant and verifiable success that can't be denied. In contrast, the right business broker isn't just going to be good, they're going to be good for you, and what this means is different for every business owner. At Business Exit Advisors, we want every business owner looking to sell their business to find the right broker for their needs and circumstances. This process includes knowing what to ask potential brokers, knowing how to vet potential brokers, knowing how brokers earn their fees, and knowing where to look in order to find a broker that is reputable.

The 3 questions to ask all business brokers

In selecting a business broker or brokerage to broker the sale of your business, there are several questions that you will want to ask. While any question you ask is valid and can help clarify the process or make you feel more comfortable, there are three questions that you must ask and have answered to your satisfaction.

1 - What's your background?

The first question to ask any broker is "What is your sales background?". It may seem redundant to ask a business broker about their work history after you've approached them, but what you're trying to find out with this question is how much practical experience they have selling businesses. The reasoning for this is that anyone who has a real estate license can also sell a business. While a broker may be good in their current role selling businesses, even if they are new at it or only working at it part time, it is unlikely that they will be as good as someone who has a proven track record of brokering business deals.

You want a business broker who not only has experience selling businesses, but also one who works for a company where that's their sole focus and where the broker has some experience with businesses in your specific industry. Business Exit Advisors only sells businesses. As a result, we've worked with sellers in a variety of different industries and we're able to use the specialized knowledge that we've gained to best help sellers find the best buyers for your specific business.

2 - *What organizations are you affiliated with?*

The second question that you want to ask any broker you're thinking about hiring is "What professional organizations are you currently affiliated with?". For example, a critical organization for business brokers in South Florida is Business Brokers of Florida (BBF). Members of BBF must demonstrate their skill as business brokers in order to be accepted and once their membership is approved, they are required to adhere to a strict code of professional ethics. Additionally, members in BBF, work together to collaborate on transactions, increasing the likelihood that a business not only sells, but that it'll sell in a timely manner, and for a fair price. Membership in organizations like BBF indicates the quality of the brokerage while affiliation isn't necessary for a broker, it does indicate what professional standards may govern their business practice.

Business Exit Advisors is not only a member in good standing of BBF but has also earned top organizational awards. We take our professional reputation seriously and work to cultivate relationships with others interested in sustained excellence. This allows us to stay on top of changing industry norms and standards in real time, which helps to create an experience for the buyer that is as straightforward as possible.

3 - How much are you going to put into marketing the business for sale?

The final question that you want to be sure to ask any business broker that you're considering working with is "How are you going to market my business?". Asking this question is important for two key reasons. First, it helps you measure what type of access they have to different marketing tools and avenues. Second, it helps you to determine what, if any, specific consideration they have given to the sale of your business and the unique needs that may have to be addressed in order to facilitate the sale.

Business Exit Advisors has access to over a dozen potential sales channels. Additionally, whenever we are hired to sell a business, we bring in professionals whose job it is to work specifically on that sale. We pride ourselves on building a team to work with each of our clients and are excited to put in the necessary efforts and funds to help make the sale of your business successful.

How to vet potential brokers for your business

Once you have found a brokerage that you think you want to work with, the next step is to vet the broker or brokers who are going to be responsible for your sale. There is unfortunately no universal or foolproof way to do this, which reinforces why the questions you should ask a potential broker are so important in the first place. If you do your due diligence in this regard, being sure to ask follow-up and clarification questions as necessary, then it is likely that you will end up hiring a broker who is well-suited to selling your business.

How good brokers earn their fees

How a company earns its fees can be an indirect indicator of the quality of work that you will ultimately receive from them. While deposits, retainers, and payment plans are standard across many different industries, these policies should give you pause if they are brought up in the context of brokering a business sale. This may indicate that the broker is not as motivated to sell your business as they are to line up as many different businesses for sale to receive as many deposits as possible. This certainly will not be the case with all business brokers and every brokerage will structure their fee schedules in a way that makes the most sense for them. It is, however, an issue worth noting, especially when compared with brokers who don't receive any fee until after the deal is closed.

Business Exit Advisors earns our fee by selling your business. What this means is that we don't get paid until you get paid, and our fee; isn't money that you're paying directly out of pocket, it will be a portion of the sale price. Pricing in this way incentivizes taking the steps necessary to ensure as smooth a sales process as possible. In some instances, this may involve co-brokering, or working with other brokers on the sale. This process may reduce the amount of money that our Company makes but will increase the chances that your business is not only sold in a timely manner, but also sold for an asking price that you're comfortable with. We are glad to organize our fees like this because we never want our potential commission to get in the way of a possible sale.

How to find a reputable broker

Finding a reputable broker is a fairly simple process. However, just because it isn't complicated doesn't mean that it may not take some time. Two of the best ways to find a reputable broker include searching for an agent via the website of a professional business broker organization or via a referral from someone you know who has already gone through the process of selling their business.

If you're completely unsure about where to start looking for a reputable broker, one of the best places to start is on the websites of organizations like the International Business Brokers Association (IBBA.org). Via this website it's possible to search for an agent by name to see if they're a member in good standing of the group. This can be especially helpful if you meet a broker who claims to be affiliated with a specific organization and you want to further vet them, checking the veracity of their claim. Additionally, members of these professional organizations are often held to high professional standards which follows that they are likely to be more reputable than brokers who are not similarly affiliated.

Not everyone who is looking for a reputable broker starts from the beginning of the search even if it feels that way. If you know someone who has already gone through the process of selling their business and they are willing to discuss their broker experience this could be very helpful.

Considering even if they had a bad experience and aren't willing to recommend the brokerage that they worked with because of it, this information can still save you time and money by helping you to avoid hiring a broker who may not be as reputable as they appear.

Exercises for Moving Forward

When you begin the process of looking for a business brokerage to sell your business, you're going to notice that they all present in a fairly similar manner. Both individual brokers and brokerage companies are going to do their best to sell you on the idea that they're the best. What you need to keep in mind, though, is that you shouldn't necessarily be seeking out the best broker. Instead, you should be seeking out the best broker for *your* business and *your* needs. The reason for this is that as important as past successes are, your broker should be reflective of your current situation and what you're looking to achieve as a result. You may notice that some of the exercises in this section were asked for after earlier chapters. Taking the time to compare your answers can be helpful in guiding your final decision as you seek out a broker.

1. In my own words I think the role of a business broker is to _____

_____.

2. I believe that a business broker fulfills their role when they _____

_____.

3. Considering the presented 3 questions that every broker should be asked, I think the most important one is _____

_____. I think that this question is the most important because _____

_____.

4. Considering the presented 3 questions that every broker should be asked, the one that is the least important to me is _____. I'm less concerned about the answer to this question because _____.

5. Looking beyond the presented 3 questions I think the most important question to ask is _____. I think that this question is important because _____. Ideally, I want the broker to tell me _____.

6. Conduct an online search and find up to 3 *local* business brokerages. List the websites in the space below:

_____

_____

_____

7. Using only the information from websites found for question 6, the brokerage that seems the most reputable is _____. I think this brokerage is the most reputable because _____.

8. Focusing on the brokerage from question 7, which, if any, professional business brokerage agencies do they belong to _____.

Do you know someone who has successfully sold their business? Connect with them to complete exercise 9.

9. Ask the person you know who sold their business the following questions:

The business was sold in _____

What industry was the business in? _____

What type of business was it (e.g. Mainstreet)? _____

How was the business owned (e.g. sole proprietor)? _____

How much did the business sell for? _____

Was the sale price more or less than the asking price? _____

How long did the sale take? _____

What business brokerage was used? _____

What factors made the experience positive? _____

_____

What factors made the experience negative _____

_____

Would they recommend the business brokerage that they used, why or why not? _____

_____

Finding the right business brokerage to handle the sale of your company is critical. You must trust that whoever you hire is going to work with you, and that they're going to respectfully represent you and your interests in all negotiations. Keeping this reality in mind, make sure that you take the time you need to make this decision.

Now that you understand what it takes to find the right broker, focus can be placed on following through with the art of sale. It's at this point in the process of preparing to take your business to market that you and your selected team will begin to make the more concrete decisions that will help transform "For Sale" into "Sold".

The Art of the Sale

Now that you're aware selling a business is a process like any other process, there are specific steps that you need to take, and whenever possible, missteps and mistakes that you want to avoid. Keeping this in mind, it can be incredibly helpful to have a clear idea of what you need to do to move closer to getting your business sold.

This section will focus on what you need to have in place to confidently have a broker take your business to market and ideally transform your "For Sale" sign into one that reads "Sold". Keep in mind as you read through this chapter that what you'll learn is a broad overview of what you can expect when working with Business Exit Advisors, and that the advice of different brokers and brokerages may differ. Please know that Business Exit Advisors has successfully used the following processes and we would be happy to have more in-depth discussions with you regarding your specific needs. When you're finished reading this section you'll have insight on the following topics:

- Taking your business to market.
- Finding the right buyer.
- Closing the deal on the sale of your business.

7. TAKING YOUR BUSINESS TO MARKET

"It's not what you sell that matters as much as how you sell it!" - Brian Halligan

If you've gotten this far in the book you know that taking your business to market is more complicated than just listing the business for sale online or in your local paper, especially if you're looking to get maximum value for it. Based on this, it should be no surprise that taking a business to market is a multi-step process that should be carefully followed in order to minimize the possibility that your business takes longer than average to sell. It would be impossible to share with you absolutely everything necessary to take your business to market because there's no universal plan that works for every single business owner or every single business. However, there are some steps that Business Exit Advisors takes in every scenario to help ensure your success as a seller when you embark on the process of taking your business to market.

The very first step you need to take

The good news is that you've already taken the first step towards taking your business to market. By picking up this book and working your way through the chapters and their exercises, you've begun preliminary work to prepare yourself and your business for sale. Next, you'll have to be proactive in presenting that business to a brokerage so that they can begin the sales process which starts with marketing.

Whether you're looking to sell your business in the next year or in the next five years, the sale is going to hinge largely on how and to whom its marketed. Business Exit Advisors offers an initial complimentary consultation to help address your specific business needs. Even if you're not ready to sell your business right now but you know that you're looking to sell it in the future, it would benefit you to take advantage of this option. This will allow you to get a realistic idea of what it may truly take to sell your business. Once we have met, if you're satisfied with what we've presented, we can sign a marketing agreement and the more in-depth work of getting your business to market can begin.

Developing an Executive Summary and Confidential Information Memorandum (CIM)

No matter who you are, or how popular or profitable your business is, prospective buyers are going to have questions. Business Exit Advisors likes to have as many buyer questions as possible answered in advance. We accomplish this by developing an Executive Summary and CIM for your business, once a marketing agreement is signed.

An Executive Summary and CIM will serve as a business bio for interested buyers. This is an extensive package of information put together by Business Exit Advisors to share with potential buyers based on a questionnaire we provide to our sellers. The purpose of this questionnaire is twofold. First, it allows sellers to share all the pertinent information pertaining to their business in a single, easy to reference document. Second, it prevents the need for potentially constant phone calls or emails every time a prospective buyer has a question about you or your business. This questionnaire is specifically designed to be a time saver which will help to ensure that your business is on the market and eventually sold, as quickly and efficiently as possible.

Keep in mind that while the executive summary and CIM are designed to capture answers to the most common questions, there are some buyer questions that can't be predicted. This may be especially true if your type of business is especially niche, or it operates within a new industry. Additionally, there will be times when buyers may need or want something within the package clarified. If this is the case, Business Exit Advisors will contact you for the additional information.

Cleaning up all outstanding non-transferable debt

It is not uncommon for a business to carry some debt during its operations. While some of this debt may ultimately be transferable to the seller, such as a lease on certain assets, it's important to understand that all debt carried by a business doesn't fall into this category. It's for this reason that, following the signing of the marketing agreement and the completion of the Executive Summary and CIM, sellers focus on taking care of any non-transferable debt.

How to resolve non-transferable debt

The specific steps a seller will take to resolve their non-transferable debt will depend on their specific situation. Based on the actual amount of the debt and/or the personal assets held by the business owner, it may be possible to simply pay off any outstanding debt either in cash or by using credit at closing. This may be an especially viable option for a small business that needed to take out a microloan to cover an emergency or for a business owner with a substantial net worth. However, this is obviously not always a viable option and as such, alternatives for paying down that debt may need to be explored. Based on the seller's specific circumstances, options may include selling off assets that won't have an overly adverse impact on the valuation of the business and/or taking out a personal loan to pay off the business debts. Such decisions should not be made lightly, and should be discussed not only with your broker, but with anyone directly impacted, such as a spouse or a dependent adult child.

What happens if non-transferable debt can't be cleared in advance?

If, for whatever reason, a seller is unable to clear up non-transferable debt prior to their business closing, this generally isn't impactful on the sale. Instead, at closing a percentage of the sale price will be allocated to paying off any remaining debt. This option can be favorable in a variety of scenarios. For example, it can be helpful in cases where a sale is being expedited for some reason and it's not possible to clear up the debt in the same time frame. Similarly, it can be helpful in instances where for whatever reason, a business owner is unable or unwilling to expend additional financial resources or take on new debt prior to the sale of their business.

Getting SBA pre-qualified

One of the final steps you can take to market your business is to meet with a lender (like the SBA) to have the business valued and, pre-qualified for a loan. Doing this not only offers another valuation which may be helpful when pricing the business, but it can also be attractive to potential buyers as well, because it helps to demonstrate not only the value, but also the viability of the business, at least in the short-term. This also shows the buyer that if they have a need for a loan, the business is viewed as an acceptable risk.

Exercises for Moving Forward

Finally taking your business to market can, and in many cases does, represent an exciting time for most sellers. While a qualified business broker will complete the bulk of the work associated with this part of the process, there is still a clear role that sellers directly play in this regard. By taking the time to prepare for that role properly and thoroughly, you can help to ensure that this part of the process goes as smoothly as possible.

1. Go back to section 1 of the book *So you think you can sell? pt. 1* and carefully look over the exercises completed for each chapter. Are there any responses that you would change? If so, why would you change them? If not, why would the answers remain the same? On a separate piece of paper, or in a black document file, write or type any altered answers.

2. Go back to section 2 of the book *Before the "For Sale"* and carefully look over the exercises completed for each chapter. Are there any responses that you would change? If so, why would you change them? If not, why would the answers remain the same? On a separate piece of paper, or in a black document file, write or type any altered answers.

3. Locate the websites for 3 business brokerages online that offer complimentary consultations. Schedule and complete an appointment with each one, then complete the following statements:

The business brokerage that I felt the best fit _____

_____. I feel this way about them because _____

_____.

The most important takeaway from my consultation with them was

_____.

The business brokerage that felt was the least likely to fit my needs/wants

was_____. I feel this way because

_____. While I do not

think they would be the best fit for me, one thing I learned from my

consultation with them was _____.

4. Visit www.MyExitPlan.com, schedule, and complete a complimentary consultation with Business Exit Advisors. Once complete, answer the following statements, keeping in mind, the 3 brokerages from the previous question:

Rank all 4 of the consulted business brokerages with scores from 1-4, with one being the most likely to receive my business and 4 being the least likely to receive my business:

1. _____

2. _____

3. _____

4. _____

The brokerage I placed at number 1 was ranked that way because _____
_____.

The brokerage I placed at number 4 was ranked that way because _____
_____.

It would be possible for the rankings to change if _____
_____.

5. Carefully think about your business in its present condition. Is there anything about it that in your opinion may complicate the sale? If so, what is it? _____
_____
_____.

6. Carefully consider your current needs and wants as a seller. Are there any special considerations that a business broker should be aware of? If so, what are they? _____
_____
_____.

7. My business currently has the following debt obligations: _____
_____
_____
_____

8. Looking at the debt obligations listed above which debts may be transferred to the new owner: _____

_____

_____

I think/know these debts are transferable to the new owner because

_____

_____. If these debts are not transferable to the new owner, I can clear the debt by _____

_____, This is a feasible solution because _____

_____ **OR** I will not be able to clear these debts because _____.

9. Looking at the debt obligations listed in question 7, which debts may be non-transferable to the new owner: _____

_____

_____.

I think/know these debts are non-transferable because _____

_____.

10. Out of the steps presented to take a business to market I think that the *easiest* one for my business will be _____

because _____.

However, if there is a complication with this step it may be because of

_____.

11. Out of the steps presented to take a business to market I think that the *hardest* one for my business will be _____

because _____.

However, it may be possible to make this step easier to get through by

_____.

     It is obvious that the sale of a business can't be completed without that business first being taken to market. A qualified business broker will make this part of the process as easy as possible for a potential seller with the intention of setting the stage for a sale that leaves all parties satisfied. Being prepared to work with your chosen broker by answering their questions and, depending on the situation, anticipating information that they may need but may not immediately known to ask for because it's unique to your situation, serves as an amazing starting point.

    Now that you understand the standard steps that Business Exit Advisors requires to take a business to market, let's focus on what's necessary to find the right buyer.

8. FINDING THE RIGHT BUYER

"The buyer is entitled to a bargain. The seller is entitled to a profit. So, there is a fine margin in between where the price is right. I have found this to be true to this day whether dealing in paper hats, winter underwear or hotels." - Conrad Hilton

Finding the right buyer for your business is a lot like finding the right business broker to handle your sale. While there may be a number of willing buyers, there will ultimately only be one that you choose to sell to. This choice is likely going to be based on a myriad of factors both logical and emotional. This is especially true if you're planning on either remaining temporarily employed by the business during a transition period, if you have real property that you've agreed to lease as opposed to sell, or if you'll be retaining the rights to IP but allowing the buyer to license it. Keeping this in mind, there isn't one universal formula for selecting the right buyer, but there are things that you can do to help ensure that you're happy with the outcome of the process. This will include exploring various channels to find a buyer, knowing how to vet a potential buyer, and taking steps to identify the perfect buyer for your business.

Going where the buyers are

Realistically, a potential buyer for your business can be found almost anywhere. However, the more places you look, the less likely you may be to find who you're looking for. The reason for this is all about numbers; the broader your search, the more people there will be to potentially buy your business. However, not everyone will be interested in, or capable of, buying your business so these larger pools of people aren't helpful. Based on this information, Business Exit Advisors suggests narrowing the search to specific online outlets, connecting with prospective buyers via direct mailers, or using a grassroots approach. Each of these options has clear pros and cons based on the specific business that's being sold, and the goals of the seller.

Connecting with buyers online

One of the most common ways to connect with prospective buyers is by utilizing an online platform of some kind. The specific platform(s) that the business is advertised on will be dependent on a number of factors. These factors may include the number of other businesses in the same industry listed on the site, how successful the platform has been in the past connecting buyers with sellers interested in the opportunity that is being offered, whether restrictions have been placed on how quickly the business needs to be sold, and of course the cost to advertise.

A key benefit of connecting with potential buyers online is that it allows the business to be presented in a way that strongly protects its anonymity and that of the seller, while still highlighting the benefits of purchasing it. For example, instead of naming the company for sale outright, focus can be placed on selling points, such as its' longevity in a particular industry. This can serve to entice potential buyers while still protecting the value of the company if its sale hasn't yet been publicly announced.

Another key benefit of connecting with potential buyers online is the size of the prospective pool of buyers who will be able to see the business for sale. The sheer quantity of people who may see the advertisement increases the possibility that the number of interested parties will be high. This can be especially true for businesses that operate in popular, emerging, or trending industries.

Additionally, connecting with potential buyers online removes geographic restrictions. Anyone, anywhere in the world, having access to the internet and to these websites, will be able to see your business for sale. This will greatly increase the number of potential buyers for your business.

While there are many benefits to connecting with buyers online, this does not mean that there are not potential drawbacks as well. One drawback is that because this is a common method for selling businesses, based on your industry or when you're choosing to sell, there could be a lot of competition from similar businesses being advertised. Competition isn't inherently a bad thing, however the more options that potential buyers have, the more time it may take for them to make a final decision.

Connecting with buyers via direct mailers

Taking the time to connect with buyers via direct mailers is rarely, if ever, a strategy that is used on its own. Instead, it's often used in conjunction with other methods. For example, direct mailers may be sent as a precursor to, or a follow-up after, telemarketing.

One key benefit of utilizing direct mailers is that this method is a form of strategic contact, because this method involves reaching out to potential buyers who have been identified either as being a good fit for your business or being specifically interested in the business for sale. This method can be positive, because it works by targeting buyers and may in turn streamline the sales process.

Another key benefit of utilizing direct mailers is that they can be incredibly beneficial for more niche businesses. Businesses that are highly specialized in some way or those in micro-industries, may have a better chance of reaching interested buyers through direct mailings. The parties who are identified for contact in this manner by Business Exit Advisors will be those that our brokers believe will have a strong interest in purchasing your business.

While direct mailers represent a strategic way to contact potential buyers there is a key drawback that cannot be ignored. Based on their format, direct mailers are sent out in limited quantities, and they're only sent to a select group of individuals. This limits the number of potential buyers that have access to the knowledge that your business is for sale.

Using grassroots efforts to connect with buyers

Connecting with buyers at a grassroots level is essentially the process of contacting them personally. Based on location this may include reaching out to a prospective buyer in person. However, in other instances, it may involve connecting with them over a video call or via a phone call.

One key benefit of connecting with a buyer in this way is that it conveys a personal touch. This can go a long way in helping a potential buyer to feel more at ease with the sales process, because when someone is courted personally, it can help them to feel special which may make them more likely to be receptive to the opportunity that is being presented to them.

An additional benefit of utilizing this method is that it can help a business broker gauge the interest of a potential buyer in real time. Unlike online platforms or direct mailers which are more hands-off ways of connecting buyers and sellers, taking a grassroots approach is one-on-one and allows for an immediate exchange of information. This can be incredibly beneficial, especially if the buyer being approached is someone who is more likely to respond better to direct personal communication.

One drawback to this type of connection is that to be truly effective it shouldn't occur in a vacuum. Unlike connecting with buyers online or connecting with them via direct mailers, the grassroots approach should be used as a matter of follow-up. As such it will only occur after other means of communication have taken place. Based on the perspective of the buyer, this may make them question the value of the business or cause them to wonder why they are being approached multiple times. Business Exit Advisors always works to mitigate this possible perception.

Business Exit Advisors: Successfully connecting buyers and sellers

Making connections with buyers only serves to represent half of the equation necessary to find the right buyer for a business. The other half of the equation involves making a successful connection between buyers and sellers. Business Exit Advisors understand that even if both parties are clearly interested in working together, there is often a need for at least 2 different types of meetings to take place.

The first meeting between someone seeking to sell their business and a buyer who has expressed interest is introductory in nature. At Business Exits Advisors, we schedule and host these meetings via Zoom with the purpose of allowing both parties to interact with each other in a low stakes, low pressure environment. During this time, it's possible for questions to be freely asked, for any necessary clarifications to be made, and for some initial vetting to be completed.

The second meeting between the seller and an interested buyer is an in-person meeting. At Business Exit Advisors, we schedule and host these meetings at our office either before we open in the morning or after we close for the evening. This meeting is conducted outside of regular business hours because it allows for greater confidentiality and helps to limit the possibility that someone who shouldn't be privy to the deal will become aware of it.

Recognizing the right buyer for your business

The individual or company that ultimately ends up being the right buyer for your business may be exactly who you imagine it will be. However, it is equally possible that the right buyer will be completely different. This is because the right buyer for your business is the one that allows for a successful negotiation leading to a sale. For this reason, it helps not to have too many preconceived notions about who the buyer should be: This will help you to work in good faith with your broker and understand that their focus is on ensuring that you aren't displeased with their work, in general, or with the details of the sale, in particular.

Exercises for Moving Forward

A business isn't sold until, or unless, a buyer is found for it. However, there is a difference between finding a buyer, and finding the *right* buyer. Business Exit Advisors strives to do the latter by working diligently to represent not just the business owner, but also the transaction itself. Understanding that the sale is the end goal, it's helpful for business owners to have a realistic perspective of this part of the process.

1. Based on the type of business that I have I think that the most effective way to connect with potential buyers would be via the _____ approach. I think that this approach is the best for my business because

_____.

2. Based on the type of business that I have I think that the *least* effective way to connect with potential buyers would be via the _____ approach. I think that this approach wouldn't work for my business because _____.

3. In making a connection with a potential buyer I would like the introductory meeting to cover _____

_____.

_____.

This is important to me because_____

_____.

4. In making a connection with a potential buyer I would like a face to face meeting to cover _____

_____.

This is important to be because _____
_____ .

5. In my opinion the right buyer for my business would be _____
_____ because _____ .
I'm basing this assessment on _____ .

6. I would be most open to a buyer who could meet the following
conditions: _____
_____ . These
conditions are important to me because _____
_____ .

       Finding the right buyer for your business is the goal for Business Exit Advisors. With every sale, it is our hope that the new owner of the business will be as successful, hopefully more successful than the former owner, and that the legacy of the business will continue in some tangible way. This is why we work diligently to ensure that the business is ultimately sold to the individual or company that will be the best overall match.

       Now that you understand the standard steps that Business Exit Advisors takes to find the right buyer for your business, focus can be placed on the process of ultimately closing the deal.

9. CLOSING THE DEAL

"Expect the yes. Embrace the no. That's how you master the close!" Unknown

Finding a buyer for your business does not conclude either the work for your business broker or the transaction as a whole, although it may initially seem as if that's the case. It's important to note that no business is sold until the deal is officially closed. This part of the sales process can seem deceptively simple when taken at face value, because by this point in the sale much of the important leg work has already been completed. However, Business Exit Advisors feels that no deal is considered complete until all appropriate paperwork has been signed and there is payment in hand. For this reason, we put as much attention into the aspects of the sale that are directly necessary for closing the deal as we do to every other part of the sales process.

Due Diligence

The first step in the two-part process necessary to close on the sale of your business involves performing the final due diligence. This is where we present the information and documentation of your business and financial history to a buyer and seek answers to any questions that arise during the review of such data. It is at this point where Business Exit Advisors, becomes a conduit of information between the buyer and seller and converts to a transactional representative.

By working on behalf of the transaction, Business Exit Advisors will be communicating what the buyer needs from the seller and will aid the seller in providing this information in a timely manner. Also, during this part of the process, final clarification is obtained by both parties, and everyone needs to be in a position where they are comfortable moving forward with the sale.

Based on the importance of conducting due diligence, it is important to note that this part of the process isn't completed in a few hours or even a few days. Instead, based on factors including the size of the business and how the deal is being financed, it can take between thirty and one hundred and twenty days to complete. While this may seem like a long period, all of this time is necessary in order to ensure that there are no surprises when the full deal is finally closed.

Landlord and other lease and license negotiations

The second and final step in the two-part deal closing process will be to handle landlord lease negotiations. Half of all otherwise solid deals are killed at this point. It's for this reason that Business Exit Advisors considers these negotiations critical to how successful a final deal is when finally closed.

Landlord negotiations

In any scenario where the business being sold has a physical location with real estate that isn't owned by the seller, it is necessary for negotiations to be conducted with the landlord or leaseholder. It shouldn't be presumed that a landlord will be open to accepting a new tenant under the same terms as the current business leasing agreement. This is true even when the business conducted at that location will be the same or in situations where the buyer of the business plans to immediately occupy the space and there will be no lapse in rent. Landlords may be leery about accepting any tenant that they did not initially vet, or in the case of businesses that have occupied the same space for years with little to no increase in their rent, landlords may view new incoming tenants as an opportunity to significantly raise the rent. Additionally, some landlords may only be willing to transfer the lease if certain conditions are met, such as the payout of an additional security deposit or a request that the current business owner stay on the lease for an agreed upon amount of time. While these all represent key changes to the lease agreement, Business Exit Advisors has found that it is best not to approach a landlord about their lease agreements too early in the process. Instead, we will not approach them until a closing date for the sale of the business has been set. A part of the rationale for this is that while it gives them some time to consider what they may want in regard to new lease terms, it also provides them with a clear time frame in which to share this information. We also will never introduce a potential buyer to a landlord until they have signed off on due diligence and the seller's security deposit has been evaluated.

Other lease and licensing negotiations

While negotiating with a landlord can be a daunting part of the process from the perspective of both buyers and sellers, it can be more straightforward than dealing with some of the other companies holding lease or asset licenses that your business may rely on to be fully operational. Based on your specific business, this may include specialty equipment that your business is leasing and/or any IP that is licensed by a third party. Ideally, these leases and licenses can be transferred with comparable terms, however, there are instances when this may not be the case. In these scenarios, Business Exit Advisors will work to ensure that the terms requested by the lease or license holders are fair for all parties involved and don't end up hindering the sale.

A special note for businesses where licensing is necessary

If you're the owner of a business such as a bar, hotel, or a location that provides adult entertainment, then you're already fully aware that these locations require special licensing (such as liquor licenses). You also may be aware that such licensing generally does not transfer once a business is sold and thus any new owner looking to run your business in the same or similar capacity will need to obtain these licenses in their own names. This reality can prolong, or even prevent the closing of a deal, based on the outcome of whether the party interested in buying the business is eligible for, or otherwise able to obtain, the necessary licensing. While information regarding eligibility will be determined in advance during the vetting stage, it may be outside of the control of the prospective buyer whether they are able to obtain the licensing in a timely manner based on the specific Municipality, County, City, or State where the business is located. Business Exit Advisors will always work to get clear timelines regarding licensing to help mitigate the possibility of the sale not closing.

Exercises for Moving Forward

Finally, closing the deal for the sale of your business can, understandably, be the most exciting part of the entire process as a seller. However, this doesn't, and can't, occur without some additional work on the part of your broker to ensure that everything about the transaction is honest and able to proceed as smoothly as possible. As the seller, there are some things that you can do to help to mitigate the possibility of negative issues delaying or even derailing the closing of the sale.

1. Looking objectively at your business as-is, do you think that there are any potential questions that may arise from a prospective seller? If so, list those questions below: _____

_____

_____

_____

_____

If you generated a list of questions for exercise 1, proceed to exercise 2. If you didn't generate a list of questions for exercise 1, skip to exercise 3.

2. Looking objectively at each of the questions generated for exercise 1 consider a succinct way that they could be answered. Record those answers below: _____

_____

_____

_____

_____

3. If your business currently leases real estate for any purpose, locate those leases, and determine if you can find out whether there are any provisions in the lease that you notice regarding the transfer of the lease. If so, what does that provision say verbatim? Write out the provision in full here:

_____

_____.

4. If your business currently leases equipment, vehicles etc. that are integral to its operation locate the leases, to determine if there are any provisions in the lease that you notice regarding the transfer of the lease. If so, what does that provision say verbatim? Write the provision in full here: _____

_____.

5. If your business currently licenses anything integral to its operations, locate the licenses to determine if there are any provisions in the lease regarding the transfer of the license. If so, what does that provision say verbatim? Write the provision in full here: _____

_____.

6. If your business operates in an industry where there are special licenses that are integral to its operations, recall the process that you had to go through to obtain the license(s) and note the time frame to receive the final document. Write that information in full below and indicate the year that you received the license(s): _____

Closing the deal is, understandably, the most satisfying aspect of the business sales process for many people. Knowing this is the case,

Business Exit Advisors works to make this aspect of the sale as smooth as possible. The closing can be immensely helped by working with both buyers and sellers must be cognizant that the sale will not be completely finalized until all outstanding questions are answered, and all negotiations are completed with third-party lease and license holders and/ or were agencies. It's for this reason that patience is always appreciated as Business Exit Advisors works to ensure that everyone walks away from the sale satisfied. Now that you understand what it takes to make a sale in general, and how a deal closing works in particular, it's possible to ask the question "So you think you can sell?" one final time.

SO, YOU THINK YOU CAN SELL? PT. 2

Now that you're aware of what it takes to sell a business it will be helpful to assess whether or not it's a process that you're truly ready to undertake at this time. If after that reflection, you decide that you're truly ready to move forward, then you'll be happy to know that there are things that you can do to not only make the sale go more smoothly but also help protect yourself and your assets once the sale has been completed.

This section will focus on getting your business sold in a way that helps you feel secure throughout the process, and what steps you should take once you've actually sold your business. When you're finished reading this section, you'll have knowledge on the following subjects:

- How to think like a potential buyer.
- What you need to do in order to build the best team for you to sell your business.
- How to secure the monies you receive from the sale of your business.

10. THINKING LIKE A BUYER

"You can never go too far wrong by thinking like a customer who's new to the business." - Richard Branson

One of the most critical, but too often overlooked, aspects of selling your business is taking the time to think like a potential buyer. As the seller, you likely already have a clear idea of what you want from the transaction. However, it's also important to consider the perspective of the individual making the purchase. While it's impossible to know everything that a buyer may be interested in, it is possible to take the time to consider the factors that may be of particular importance to them. Specifically, all business owners need to focus on 5 core areas. This includes the quality of their records, the asking price of the business as it may relate to a differing valuation of the business, the asking price of the business as it relates to exactly what is included in the sale, the asking price of the business as it relates to the assets associated with the business and buyer needs, and market growth potential as it relates to the scalability of the business. For business owners selling turn-key operations, there are two additional areas of focus which include brand reputation and its relationship to customer retention and growth and the current owner's attitude as it relates to employee relations. In looking at these different areas from the perspective of a potential buyer, you may realize that there are aspects of your offering that need to be altered in order to help facilitate a quicker or smoother sale.

Assessing the quality of your records

The importance of quality record-keeping simply can't be overstated. As the current business owner, you know what's in your records, however what you need to keep in mind is that a potential buyer will be seeing them for the first time after expressing an interest in your company. By the time you're ready to take your business to market, your records should have already been thoroughly evaluated and your business broker should have worked with you and your accountant or financial team to ensure that they are not only as complete as possible, but also as easy to understand as possible.

If you were the buyer, you'd want to be able to review records from the seller that are logically ordered, well-organized, and complete. Things like gaps in the record keeping, unclear profit sources, or accounting mistakes would understandably serve as red flags. Even if offered an explanation, the buyer may be unwilling to further entertain buying the business altogether or if still interested, they may attempt to negotiate a significantly reduced sales price or may want additional concessions made to move forward.

Effectively, being able to review well-kept records can help to give prospective buyers peace of mind. This will eliminate guess work and provide them with access to facts to be used as a reference going forward. The more comfortable a prospective buyer is when reviewing your records, the more comfortable they may be to ultimately pay your asking price.

Asking price vs. differing valuations

As presented in chapter 4, there isn't a one-size-fits all approach to valuing a business, instead there are various methods and models that can be utilized, all of which ultimately assign your business value. Someone looking to purchase your business may choose to conduct a valuation of their own. While as the seller you certainly don't have to agree with the outcome of this valuation, you need to be aware that it may directly influence the offer that you ultimately receive.

Know that as the seller, you've approached the process of business valuation from the position of maximizing its' worth, this is not the way the buyer will look at the situation. The buyer will be considering aspects of your business that decrease its value to use this information as leverage when negotiating the purchase price. It is for this reason that you need to look at your business objectively and consider anything and everything that may adversely impact its perceived or actual value in the eyes of the buyer.

In much the same way that you want to get the most money from the sale of your business, a buyer wants to ensure that they are getting the best value for their money and in some instances, this may mean looking for every opportunity to get a "better" deal. One method might be to present an alternate value for your business to see if you're willing to be flexible regarding the asking price. If, in advance, you're aware of what may cause the valuations to differ and potentially the difference between the two valuations, then you place yourself in a much better position to address the issues head on. Make sure to discuss any issues with your broker, so that they will be informed during negotiations on your behalf.

Asking price vs. what's included in the sale

Sellers often have a significant amount of leeway when it comes to deciding what they will and won't include when selling their business. While buyers can try to negotiate for a different price or for different terms outright, the seller is under no obligation to meet these requests, especially if they have multiple offers that are comparable and above, at, or at least close to the asking price. Such an arrangement is one that clearly favors the seller and can make potential buyers reluctant to show interest in a particular business if they feel the price being asked is too high for what they'd be receiving from the sale.

As mentioned, a buyer wants to ensure that they're receiving the most value for their money. In much the same way that this may lead you to seek an alternate valuation to justify an offer that's lower than your asking price, it may also lead the buyer to question whether what you're including as part of the sale is worth the price. While you're certainly free to disagree on matters of price versus value, it does benefit you to look objectively at what you're offering for sale and how it may be perceived by a potential buyer.

It's likely that at some point in your life you've been in a situation where you didn't feel the price being asked for a product, service, or experience was in complete alignment with what you were going to receive. While it's possible in this situation you may willingly pay the price, it's just as likely that in doing so there may be an emotional cost. Similarly, you may choose not to pay the price at all, and instead seek out something that's comparable somewhere else. This is the position that you put a buyer in when there's a disconnect between the price being asked and what's actually being received in return. By being proactive, thinking about, and most importantly, working to ensure a happy medium between the price you're asking and what a buyer getting, you may minimize the need for negotiation which can in turn help to expedite the sales process.

Asking price vs. assets

In many ways the assets that are associated with a business *are* the business itself. For example, it would be impossible for soft drink companies to sell their products without access to their bottling plants, the efficiency of a restaurant hinges largely on the quality of their kitchens, and amusement parks are able to attract visitors based on the rides that they offer. Similarly, things like proprietary software can be integral to the competitive advantage of a technology company and the iconic nature of specific characters or properties are essential to the ongoing profitability of movie studios and some streaming services. The assets a business holds can play a clear role in valuation and are of primary interest to potential buyers. Even if all the business assets are included in the sale, it's important to understand that potential buyers may still have questions and concerns which they may use to try to negotiate a lower purchase price.

Asking price vs. valuation of real property assets and buyer needs

It should not be automatically assumed that an abundance of real property assets means that your asking price will be paid without question. What needs to be considered are both the value of those assets as well as what exactly the buyer needs. While you can, and should, have the former professionally calculated, the latter may not be immediately apparent unless, or until, you enter negotiations with the buyer.

When considering the price that you're asking for your business and the assets that are included in the sale, the buyer is most likely going to be focused on the quality of those assets as well as their need for them. For example, imagine the business for sale is a car dealership with the lot, associated buildings, and all the inventory included, but the real estate is located in a crime ridden area and there have been prior break-ins either at the location itself or in close proximity to it. Because of this the buyer may only be interested in the inventory with the intention of selling the lot, its buildings, and relocating the business to an area that they deem more desirable. In a situation like this, the real estate can be viewed as representing a lower quality asset based on both real and perceived value and in choosing not to occupy it, the need for a new location is created in the mind of the buyer. Such a scenario may result in a buyer looking to pay lower than what's being asked, to maximize the value of their investment.

It's impossible to anticipate how every potential buyer will react to the assets being offered in conjunction with the sale of your business or how these assets will or will not be viewed in terms of helping them to meet the buyer's needs moving forward. With that said, however, there does need to be an objective review of the assets that are being included in the sale. While you may have conducted such a review during the valuation of your business, it is a good idea to revisit it with fresh eyes as if you were the buyer and not the seller. Taking the time to do this may reveal changes that you can make to either the asking price or the assets.

Asking price vs. valuation of IP

Assigning value to IP can be much more difficult than assigning value to real property. This is especially true when you're dealing with new IP, or IP that may be contested in some way as infringing on the rights of another person or company and, subsequently, may be the subject of future litigation. Thus, the sale of IP associated with your business can be just as likely to harm your asking price as it can help to enhance it.

Buyers are not interested in purchasing liabilities or in taking on losses that are viewed as being avoidable in some way. It's for this reason that you need to objectively assess your IP in terms of both its potential future viability, as well as its continued legality. While there's no way to be 100% certain, you can make an educated guess based on industry trends and the current and projected economic and legal climates. It's completely possible that the IP you own and are selling as a part of your business more than justifies the price that you're asking. If this isn't a certainty though, you may need to reconsider your asking price.

In the same way that it is impossible to anticipate the reaction of every potential buyer regarding the real property assets you're offering and how they may align with their needs, it is equally impossible to know precisely how a buyer will value the IP that you're offering. Rather than attempting, and ultimately failing, to figure this out, it's far better for you to be able to assess the value of your IP based on a valuation method that can be replicated, as opposed to your perception of the value. An accurate assessment to be shared with your broker may put you in a better position to get your asking price. An established business broker will then be able to clearly articulate value that may not be immediately obvious to the buyer.

Asking price vs. assets and turn-key operations: Leasing and licensing terms

While all businesses may have assets that they lease or license as opposed to owning outright, this takes on a different importance when looking at the sale of turn-key operations. This is because, in the event that, there are necessary leases and licenses such as those for the real estate where the business is located or copyright protected images that are strongly associated with the business which are non-transferable, the buyer will be placed in the position of negotiating new contracts.

It would be remiss to assume that the person who buys your business will have the same costs that you currently have, costs that may have been considered when the valuation for your business was completed and the asking price decided on. Keep in mind there are no guarantees that a prospective buyer will be offered the necessary leases and licenses associated with the business at the rate that you're currently paying. Based on this calculation, the buyer may seek a lower purchase price to offset these additional costs and to ensure a smooth transition between owners.

Having the understanding that whoever buys your business may need to regularly pay more to keep it operational, may influence the price that you decide to ask for it, or it may cause you to purchase assets that you're currently leasing as a way of justifying the price point. In either scenario, the act of thinking like a buyer can make you more aware of the way in which leases and licensing fees can influence the offers that you ultimately receive.

Market growth potential and business scalability

The size of the market that your business serves today may not be the size of the market that it serves tomorrow or ten years from now. Instead of remaining static, markets can, and do, shrink, or expand based in part on the scalability of a specific business. With this in mind, a savvy buyer, especially one who is looking to potentially expand, is going to be focused on whether the market for your business is one that is likely to grow and how feasible it will be for them to capitalize on it.

Not every buyer will be interested in growing your business, and you may mistakenly think that even if they are, that's none of your concern. It is your concern though, because if a buyer believes that your business can be scaled to capture a more significant market share, they're much more likely to pay what you're asking, or potentially more than what you're asking in order to acquire it. Buyers want to believe they will receive significant future returns on their investment.

While you may not have considered it before, especially if you're an owner operated business or a business owner in a niche industry, there is no harm in taking some time to think about ways your business could be scaled for greater market share and discussing this with your broker. The conversation about scalability may never arise with potential buyers, but if it does, and it's something you've thought about, it could aid in helping you and your broker close the deal.

Special considerations for turn-key operations

Based on the nature of turn-key operations, buyers looking to purchase this type of business have considerations to make that aren't relevant in asset-based purchases. Specifically, buyers may be interested in the current reputation of the business and the way in which it has, and may continue to, impact customer retention and growth. It's important for buyers to consider these factors because buying a turn-key operation is, at least in the short-term, buying a business "as-is". While in some cases this can be a good thing, in other cases it can be very bad.

Business reputation and customer retention and growth

The reputation of a business can have a significant influence on whether or not that business is able to retain its current customer base and expand its market. Businesses with positive reputations likely enjoy the loyalty of their current customers, while also having the ability to easily attract new ones. In contrast, if a business lacks a clear reputation, has an inconsistent one, or worse yet, has a bad one, the future of that business may be in jeopardy.

Buyers are not interested in purchasing problems, and a bad reputation can be highly problematic for a business, even once new ownership is announced. The reason for this is twofold. First, individuals who feel negatively about a business are unlikely to seek out updates about it, so the announcement of new owners may reach a limited audience which won't allow the new owner the opportunity to showcase how they are running it. Second, if the business has a poor reputation based on something like its employees or its location then new ownership is unlikely to be able to immediately change either of these issues. This would likely result in the persistence of a bad reputation until the new owners are able to figure out a solution.

Absolutely no business is perfect. and no buyer expects it to be, however it is unfair, and potentially detrimental to your asking price, to expect a buyer to be willing to pay for the poor reputation of a business. Therefore, if you're aware that your business has a reputation that's shaky or unfavorable, it benefits you to find ways to address the negative situation and advise your broker of potential solutions to share with prospective buyers.

Current owner attitude, actions, and employee relations

When you run a business, you can operate it in any way that you see fit. As long as you're abiding by local, state, and federal labor laws, there's nothing that anyone can do to stop you. In some instances, this means that a business owner will do the bare minimum to be legally compliant, while in other instances there are owners who will go well above and beyond for their employees, and of course, there are owners who occupy a middle ground. As long as you're in charge, the way you interact with your employees isn't likely something that you give a lot, if any, real thought to. However, when you decide that you want to sell your business as a turn-key operation, it's something that you need to seriously consider.

Unless all of your employees plan to leave when you sell your business or the buyer insists on bringing in all new people, when you sell your turn-key operation, you're effectively also selling the tone that's been set for interpersonal relationships within the company. This is significant to a buyer, because while they were not involved with the way these relationships developed, they are going to be, at least in the short term, influenced by how they have been functioning in the past. This isn't really going to be problematic if the buyer has a similar style of management to yours, but it can be a major issue if they don't.

You don't technically need to allow a prospective buyer to observe the way you interact with your employees or the way that they interact with others, and there can be a legitimate reluctance in doing so, especially if the sale of the business isn't public knowledge. However, allowing someone to see these relationship dynamics can be beneficial. For example, if you are the type of business owner who willingly and routinely provides your employees with perks and benefits that are in addition to what's in their employment contracts, showcasing this to a prospective buyer can signal that this is what your employees have come to expect. This may allow the weeding out of potential buyers not interested in, or able to, do the same things that you do. Additionally, allowing prospective buyers this type of access can generate some good will between you and them, which may help at sale time.

Exercises for Moving Forward

It's unlikely that thinking about the sale of your business from the perspective of a potential buyer was something originally on your to-do list when you considered selling it. However, taking the time to do this can be beneficial to the sales process. Thinking like a buyer puts you in the best position as a seller to minimize problems which in turn may help to maximize your profit.

1. As the business owner on a scale of 1 to 10, with 1 being the poorest quality and 10 being the highest quality, I would rate my current business records a _____. My reason for this rating is _____ _____.

If the rating is below a 10: I can increase this rating by doing the following:
_____
_____.

2. Taking on the perspective of a buyer on a scale of 1 to 10, with 1 being the poorest quality and 10 being the highest quality, I would rate my current business records a _____. My reason for this rating is _____.

If the rating is below a 10: I can increase this rating by doing the following:
_____
_____.

3. Ideally, I'd like to receive _____ (fill in the blank with the dollar amount) for my business. I think that this amount is a reasonable asking price because _____.

Refer back to the valuation models listed in chapter 4 (asset valuations, calculating liquidation value, utilizing the times revenue model, utilizing and earnings multiplier, and using the rule of thumb). Select one of those models to answer the following question:

4. Taking on the perspective of the buyer, I believe that the valuation model that would offer me the most leverage when making an offer on the business would be _____ because _____
_____.

5. As the seller of the business I would challenge the valuation based on the model selected for question for by _____
_____. This challenge is a valid counter to this valuation because _____
_____.

6. As the business owner I feel that my asking price of _____ is justified based on what is included in the sale because _____
_____.

7. Taking on the perspective of the buyer the asking price of _____ would be justified based on what is included in the sale because _____ _____**OR** would not be justified based on what is included in the sale because _____ _____. As the seller I can work to better justify this price by _____ _____.

8. As the business owner I feel that my asking price of _____ is justified based on the value of my real property assets because _____ _____.

9. Taking on the perspective of the buyer the asking price of _____ would be justified based on the value of my real property assets because _____

OR would not be justified based on the value of my real property assets because_____.
As the seller I can work to better justify this price by _____ _____.

10. As the business owner I feel that my asking price of _____ is justified based on the value of my IP because _____ _____.

11. Taking on the perspective of the buyer the asking price of _____ would be justified based on the value of my IP because _____ **OR** would not be justified based on the value of my IP because _____. As the seller I can work to better justify this price by _____

_____.

12. *For those looking to sell turn-key operations only.*
As the business owner I feel that my asking price of _____ is justified based on the current costs associated with my leases and licensing agreements because _____

_____.

I would be willing to lower my asking price to _____ if I discovered that the leases and licensing fees for the buyer would be higher **OR** I would not be willing to lower my asking price if I discovered that the leasing and licensing fees for the new owner would be higher because

_____.

13. If I was looking to scale up as opposed to sell my current business three ways which this could be accomplished could be_____

_____, _____

_____, and _____

_____.

These are feasible options for market growth because _____

_____

_____

_____.

14. *For those looking to sell turn-key operations only.*

As the business owner I feel that my asking price of _____ is justified based on the current reputation of my business because _____

_____.

15. *For those looking to sell turn-key operations only.*

Taking on the perspective of the buyer the asking price of _____ would be justified based on the current reputation of the business because_____

_____**OR** would not be justified based on the current reputation of the business because _____.

As the seller I can work to better justify this price by _____

_____.

16. *For those looking to sell turn-key operations only.*

As the business owner I feel that my asking price of _____ is justified based on the current owner/employee relationship and employee/employee relationship within my business because _____

_____.

17. *For those looking to sell turn-key operations only.*

Taking on the perspective of the buyer the asking price of _____ would be justified based on the current owner/employee relationship and employee/employee relationship within my business because _____

_____.

OR would not be justified based on the current owner/employee relationship and employee/employee relationship within my business because_____.

As the seller I can work to better justify this price by _____
_____.

Being willing to take the time to step back, looking at the business you're selling objectively, and thinking like a buyer is a key step that many sellers do not think to inherently consider. This can be a costly mistake as it can lead to an unwillingness to be flexible regarding aspects of the sale. However, taking the time to view the transaction from the perspective of the other party can lead to a greater willingness to compromise and ultimately create a better sales experience for all involved parties.

Now that you've taken the time to think like a prospective buyer you can focus on building the best team to sell your business.

11. BUILDING THE RIGHT TEAM

"Great things in business are never done by one person; they're done by a team of people." - Steve Jobs

In building the right team to facilitate the sale of your business, you need to have a core group of people who are aware of what you're going through and will allow you to work with people whose business it is to sell your business. The former group makes up your support team, while the latter group makes up your sales team. Your sales team individuals don't only need to be experts in their fields, but they should also have relevant licensing credentials, and ideally be accredited, where applicable. The reason for this is simple; when you work with the best, you're more likely to receive the best possible outcome. With this in mind, it's time to focus both on who needs to be on your support team and why Business Exit Advisors should be your sales team.

Who needs to be on your support team?

As a business owner, even if you're a sole proprietor, there's an understanding that for your business to run optimally it's not something that you can do entirely on your own. Like running your business, the process of selling your business can be at times stressful or complicated and in those moments, having a team that you can trust will be integral in helping you to remain clear headed and focused on the sale close. However, it can also be incredibly difficult to decide who should be made aware of the impending sale, and who will best support you, especially if there are unforeseen setbacks. Based on this, it's recommended that your support team be composed of two different types of people; those who absolutely need to know about the sale and can be designated as your professional support team, and a smaller group of people who will offer you emotional support throughout the process. These folks will be your personal support team.

Your professional support team

Despite its name, your professional support team does not, and should not, include everyone that currently works for you. Instead, it should include the people who work for you and with you, who absolutely need to be made aware of the fact that you are planning on selling the business. The members of this team will vary based on factors, such as what type of business you have, how your business is owned, and how many important roles and functions are outsourced.

First, for anyone other than a sole proprietor, the most important members of your professional support team will be anyone who co-owns the business or who has a stake in the sale. In cases of franchise owners, it will be the parent company. These individuals or entities will be going through the process with you which will necessitate everyone working closely together. Based on this, even if the relationships are informal, or contentious in nature, it will definitely help to come to an agreement that during the process of selling the business, you will work together for the good of the transaction. Having everyone with a claim to ownership on the same page will help the process to run smoothly.

Second, you should loop in your lawyer if you have one on retainer or one that handles your business. Since this person is someone you've worked with in the past in order to negotiate deals, they'll have quick access to your contracts, leases, etc. and will be able to help explain anything in the original documents that may be pertinent. Additionally, while Business Exit Advisors has its own legal team on staff, we understand the desire for business owners to have any new legal documents read by a lawyer with whom you already have a relationship.

Next, it will be helpful to discuss the deal with your business and personal accountant(s). This is especially necessary if you're looking to dole out severance pay for some or all of your employees, following a sale where they may lose their jobs. Your accountant should know how much money can realistically be, or already is, earmarked for this purpose. He/She should be able to offer you the best financial advice regarding how such payments can be legally structured.

Finally, you may want to bring in certain key members of your senior staff or department heads as the deal progresses. This can be especially key if the sale is being made via an asset purchase agreement and there may be employees who are adversely impacted and could lose their jobs as a result. Being able to discuss this possibility with those in upper management can help you to best determine what, if anything, may be possible for you to do in terms of helping exceptional members of your staff retain their employment.

Your personal support team

Equally, if not more, important than your professional support team, is your personal support team. You may find that there are only one or two people in your life who are truly capable of fulfilling this role as the individuals you select need to be people in your life who have proven themselves to be trustworthy. The reason for this is that selling a business can be a highly sensitive matter, especially in instances where the sale has the possibility to impact a lot of people, generate a lot of money, or will result in a very successful, or well-loved company changing ownership.

Based on this, it is imperative that whoever you decide to include on your personal support team embodies the qualities of discretion, loyalty, and compassion, as it will be necessary for them to display all these emotions during different parts of the process.

One other consideration for your personal support team is the need for someone who is going to have "your back". Like how you should be willing to think like a buyer, you need to be willing to take a moment and consider this position from the perspective of the person who you're asking to be your support. It's important to consider both what personal and professional commitments the individual in question already has to fulfill, as well as the way you generally interact with them when you're under stress. By considering what else they have going on in their lives, you can estimate how much time they may have to truly be a source of support for you while you're going through this process. Recognizing that everyone handles stress differently and that we display stress differently to different people in our life. Being honest about the way in which you showcase your stress to the people that you're considering for your personal support team, can help you determine whether or not this is a process that you actually want to include them in because it may ultimately end up putting a strain on your relationship(s).

Why Business Exit Advisors should be your sales team

Choosing the right business brokerage to serve as your sales team is a responsibility that shouldn't be undertaken lightly. Please know that Business Exit Advisors would be honored to fill this team for you.

One of the best ways to decide whether a business brokerage may ultimately be the right one to take your business to market is to consider the work that they have done for other business owners in the past or in other words, their experience. Business Exit Advisors has successfully brokered the sale of businesses for hundreds of companies in a variety of different circumstances. It would be impossible to share all our success stories in this book, however, by providing a sample, we'll be able to showcase some of the positive and profitable outcomes we've experienced.

Success Story #1: Fast moving flowers

Being a business broker often means needing to be incredibly flexible about the working conditions because it's impossible to control every aspect of the circumstances under which a business is sold. One prime example came in the form of a flower and catering company that, despite its immense success, needed to be sold suddenly and quickly. In this situation not only were we working with a tight deadline, but also with a sense of responsibility to preserve the legacy of the business.

Prior to its sale, the company had over five decades of success. During the years it initially operated, it was the go-to location for celebrities and other high net-worth individuals looking to meet their floral needs. Based on this, it was the type of company that held significant appeal and would have been an amazing acquisition for a buyer who was already in or seeking to enter into the floral industry. However, the circumstances surrounding its sale posed some unique challenges.

In this situation, the owner of the business was the sole proprietor. Like many sole proprietors of successful companies, he had dedicated his whole life to building and growing his company, and in many ways, he was the brand. While this was great in the sense that it allowed him the opportunity to cultivate a positive reputation, unfortunately, he died suddenly without a succession plan in place. As a result, his business was being sold by his estate, and they wanted it to be sold quickly. When Business Exit Advisors became involved, we knew that one of our priorities was to figure out the best way to broker the sale, knowing that its recently deceased owner was central to its success.

Looking to honor the wishes of the family for a quick sale as well as the legacy of the business owner, Business Exit Advisors focused on finding a motivated buyer who was already involved in the floral industry and local to the area. The key selling point was the established and respected nature of the business, including that there was an existing phone number that had been unchanged during the life of the business, a well-known location, and a built-in clientele. Ultimately, we found another flower shop owner that already had a significant number of weddings and needed to expand. The new buyer was able to close the sale in 3 weeks.

Success story #2: Exhibit A

While there's nothing wrong with a business brokerage that wants to specialize in brokering sales within a certain industry, Business Exit Advisors. prides itself on being able to sell any type of business. This is a claim that not only has merit but was manifested in a very interesting way. Specifically, we were asked to sell a "Dead Bodies" exhibit.

During the height of the Covid-19 pandemic many business owners needed to drastically alter their operations, shut down temporarily, or make the decision to sell. It was during this time that Business Exit Advisors was approached by the owner of a "Dead Bodies" exhibit. He was looking to retire, in part because social distancing restrictions made it impossible to run his business. Based on the unconventional nature of this business, as well as the uncertainty surrounding when or if it could be restored to its full operations, we knew that there would be a limited pool of interested, potential buyers who would understand how to maintain the exhibit or would even want to.

To find a buyer, Business Exit Advisors understood that we would need to be strategic about, not only how we positioned the business, but also who we chose to contact. By limiting our reach to parties that would most likely be interested in such a niche opportunity, we were able to find a buyer in the same broad industry as our seller. Specifically, the person who ended up purchasing the business was someone who owned a dinosaur exhibit. Their decision to purchase the "Dead Bodies" exhibit allowed them to create an ancillary business to complement their primary offering.

Success story #3: Two for one

Successful business brokers understand the importance of working with both buyers and sellers in a way that will ensure both parties feel as if they are being treated fairly and with respect. This allows the brokerage to work on either side of the deal (as needed) based on the situation without compromising the quality of the work. To this end, one sale that Business Exit Advisors was fortunate to broker included a situation where the seller of the business was also a buyer in the same deal.

The decision to sell a business isn't inherently the same as the decision to retire or otherwise leave business ownership behind. Instead, there are cases where business owners want to make the transition from one business to another. This was the type of situation that we were faced with when the owners of a pizza parlor that had been open for seventeen years decided that they wanted to sell their pizza business and open a new restaurant. In this case, they became the seller in one part of the transaction and the buyer in the other part. While this is not a traditional way to structure a business sale, it made sense in this case.

By utilizing our team and leveraging their talents and know-how, it was possible for Business Exit Advisors to successfully close the sale of the pizza parlor to new owners and get the former owners into another deal where they were able to purchase both a new restaurant and the real estate attached to it. In many ways this was a quintessential win-win scenario as both parties were happy with their deals and able to embark on new business ownership journeys.

Exercises for Moving Forward

The importance of building the right support and sales teams is a facet of the business selling process that should not be understated. By working to both identify and engage the people in your life who can offer you help during this time, and finding and hiring the right brokerage, you can potentially reduce the amount of stress that you would otherwise experience during this process.

1.Take a moment to consider the individual(s) that you would include on your *professional support team*. For each of these people complete the following form:

Name: _____

Occupation/Role in your business: _____

I think that this individual would be a good addition to my professional support team because_____.

I may have a conflict with this person if _____ but this conflict can be mitigated by _____.

2.Take and moment and consider the individual(s) that you would include on your *personal support team*. For each of these people complete the following form:

Name: _____

Relationship to you: _____

I think that this individual would be a good addition to my personal support team because _____.

I may have a conflict with this person if _____ but this conflict can be mitigated by _____.

When I'm stressed, I treat this person _____. They respond to that treatment by _____.

3. Review the success stories shared by Business Exit Advisors at the end of this chapter. What, if anything, about the information shared would influence your decision on whether or not to hire the brokerage:

_____

_____

_____

_____

4. Visit www.MyExitPlan.com . Based on your review of the site, what, if anything, presented would cause you to hire Business Exit Advisors as the brokerage to work as the sales team for your business: _____

_____

_____

_____

_____

Taking the time to select and build members of your personal and professional support teams can be just as integral to the process as choosing the right brokerage to act as your sales team. This is a process that can be overlooked to the detriment of the seller who may find themselves overwhelmed at points in the process without an outlet for discussion. It's for this reason that we encourage you to put the right team in place. Even if you never need to utilize the knowledge or emotional support that your broker can offer, it's still important for peace of mind to know that they will be available if you need them.

Now that you've taken the time to carefully consider the support teams when you're selling a business, focus will be placed on what you should do once your business is sold.

12. STARTING AT "SOLD"

"One of the greatest responsibilities that I have is to manage my assets wisely, so that they create value." - Alice Walton

Business Exit Advisors doesn't consider the process of selling a business to be over just because the deal has been closed. This is because we know that following the sale, there are additional considerations for both buyers and sellers. For the individuals and companies that have purchased the business, the next steps can be obvious because they must focus on their new purchase. What may be far less obvious are the next steps that should be taken by the person, or people, who have sold the business. Specifically, once the business has been sold, careful focus needs to be placed on Asset Protection.

What is Asset Protection?

While many business owners are well versed in the concept of Asset Protection and already have careful plans in place to protect what they've earned and acquired, this isn't true for all business owners. Based on this it's important to briefly define what Asset Protection is. Essentially, Asset Protection is exactly what it sounds like, it's the practice of protecting anything of value that a person owns. There's no universal way in which this is accomplished, and a reputable Asset Protection Attorney will work with you to develop a strategy or series of strategies that best works to protect you from losing what you've worked for and/or inherited.

The importance of Asset Protection as a business seller

When you sell a business, the profits from the sale of that business become an additional asset, and when they're unprotected, any asset can quickly turn into a liability by transforming you into a target for anyone looking to turn your closed deal into a payday for themselves. In order to avoid this, you need to be sure that you're doing whatever you can to legally protect this influx of money. Be forewarned, the typical routes you may take to protect yourself such as purchasing insurance or engaging in estate planning are not enough, especially not in the early days following the sale.

Why insurance isn't enough

One thing that you may be wondering, especially if you don't already have Asset Protection strategies in place, is why insurance will not be a sufficient form of protection. The simplest explanation is that while insurance is a form of planning, it only serves to offer you protection after something bad happens, and that protection is contingent upon whatever specific policy or plan you choose. In stark contrast, Asset Protection isn't only proactive, it also serves to protect you immediately by safeguarding what you have in the now, instead of potentially repaying a portion of it in the future.

How Asset Protection differs from estate planning

Another question that you may have, even if you are familiar with Asset Protection Planning, is how this process differs from estate planning. Estate planning is a very specific form of Asset Protection planning, and rather than offering broad protection to you while you're alive, it focuses on the way in which your assets will be allocated after your death. While this is important, it may not serve to be a sufficient way to meet your most immediate needs.

The ease and importance of protecting sales proceeds

One of the easiest ways to apply Asset Protection principles and practices following the sale of your business is to have a clear plan regarding exactly where the proceeds of the sale will go, or more aptly how your profits will be protected from potential lawsuits and future creditors. While Business Exit Advisors has Asset Protection Attorneys on staff, it will be helpful for you to have some idea as to where you want the proceeds from the sale of your business to go, as this can provide a starting point for how they'll ultimately be allocated.

It's important to understand that even if you don't immediately see the necessity of protecting the sales proceeds, you should be aware that anyone can be sued and even if the suit is decided in your favor, it can still be a drain on your time and resources. Additionally, the sad reality is that selling your business can make you vulnerable to a very specific form of litigation.

One of the most common and time-consuming lawsuits observed by Business Exit Advisors is one where the new business owner sues the former owner for fraud. This happens in situations where the new owner fails to run the business like the old owner did, resulting in a reduction of income or an increase in expenses. In scenarios like this one, the new owner may threaten litigation as a form of leverage to attempt to renegotiate the terms of the sale to get money from the original owner to cover their losses, or in some situations they may seek to back out of the deal entirely. Protecting the proceeds of the sale of the business does not prevent this from happening, but it does help to increase the likelihood that the new owner will not be unjustly enriched following their failings to run the business properly.

What type of Asset Protection is right for me?

It's likely that you're wondering what type of Asset Protection strategies would be best for you to protect your proceeds from the sale of the business. It's impossible to accurately answer that question within the context of this book as Asset Protection is something that should be personalized. For a complimentary preliminary Asset Protection Planning consultation, please feel free to visit www.AssetProtectionAttorneys.com, email Info@AssetProtectionAttorneys.com, or call (561) 953-1050.

Exercises for Moving Forward

Like some of the other concepts and ideas presented, Asset Protection for the proceeds of the sale may not have been something initially on your radar when you thought about the possibility of selling your business. However, it is something that you definitely need to think about, in order to ensure that you don't lose the money you earned, after selling your business. While every scenario will differ in some way, what remains constant is that everyone needs Asset Protection.

If you currently have an Asset Protection Plan in place complete exercise 1. If you don't currently have an Asset Protection Plan in place skip to exercise 2.

1. The strategies employed by my current Asset Protection Plan include
_____. Of these strategies I think that _____ (insert specific Asset Protection strategy) would be a good way to protect the proceeds of the sale because _____.

2. Following the sale of my business my plan for allocating the money is as follows: _____
_____
_____
_____
_____

Whether Asset Protection is already familiar or a new concept to you, it's important to take it seriously to protect the proceeds from the sale of your business. By taking the time to sit down and talk with a qualified Asset Protection Attorney, you're working to protect yourself and ensure that all the work that's been done on your behalf to get your business sold hasn't been completed in vain.

Now that you've worked your way through this book, carefully consider if you're truly ready to take the next step. If you're still uncertain, Business Exit Advisors will be happy to help you make this very important decision.

ARE YOU READY TO SELL?

Visit www.MyExitPlan.com, email Info@MyExitPlan.com, or call (561) 388-8888 today to schedule your complimentary preliminary consultation.

Made in United States
Orlando, FL
22 November 2024

54295690R00095